First Printing – Spring 2025

ISBN: 979-8-9909771-3-6

Cover Illustration by Elizabeth Mackey

Editing by Brian Klems

Proofreading by Lori Diederich

ONE WRONG TURN AT A TIME – Published by NDY Press. Printed in the United States of America

DEDICATION

This book is for my favorite husband, Rice.
Thank you for sharing this life with me
with love and support along every step of the journey
and for encouraging me to move forward
and to pick a fork already!

May we savor many more miles of giggles and wonder
as we continue to travel this journey together.

You're still the one!

· ♥ ·

"There was nowhere to go but everywhere,
So just keep on rolling under the stars." ~ Jack Kerouac

Contents

Foreword

"When you come to a fork in the road, take it." ~ *Yogi Berra*

I 'm a big believer that stories matter. This one, *One Wrong Turn at a Time,* is a coming-of-age story of sorts—the coming of age of a marriage. It's about how I, along with my favorite husband, Jim (better known as Rice), learned to roll with it, baby, through the different stages and phases and places encountered along the road of building a life together.

The book is not exactly a travelogue. And it's definitely *not* a how-to manual on marriage. You could call it a how-WE-did-it but maybe-don't-try-this-yourself book. Shoot, some might even consider it the perfect bathroom book. You know, the kind of book you tuck in the loo for a quick read or two while you're passing time . . . for one reason or another.

The impetus to write the book *did* spring from our travel experiences. It was also influenced by the pandemic, which hit exactly when we retired, thwarting immediate plans to see more of Europe. As U.S. travel began to open up again, we looked at our opportunities stateside. That's when we realized we'd visited more than forty of our fifty United States together. And we had a thought: Why not go for visiting all fifty . . . and write about our experiences to boot?

The thing is, while travel provided a structure for our Fifty-State Project, the book quickly became about so much more. After all, travel choices for all of us come about based on whether we're coupled or single, if we have kids (or dependent parents), and where we are with our careers. I felt comfortable sharing this travel-adjacent information, but did Rice?

I could only ask him: "Are you cool if I go a bit deeper with our Fifty-State Project and speak on your behalf about our adventures through the years?"

His response: "Honey, you've never checked with me before. So why start now?"

Touche.

One Wrong Turn at a Time chronicles our journey so far, which *has* encompassed all fifty states and almost as many years, if dating counts. It follows two starry-eyed college sweethearts who married, moved across the country, started a family, moved again, and somehow—knock on wood—forty-plus years later and counting, are growing old together.

Dare I say, we had no clue?!

Because, as I've said, stories matter, together we rehashed some of our travel and life experiences so I could record our memories. *Our* stories. My hope is that our kids and grandkids, friends and loved ones might one day pause to read our stories and find themselves smiling.

As for you, dear reader, I'd love to think you might also savor and enjoy these stories. Perhaps you'll chuckle at seeing yourself on some of the pages. (Or breathe a sigh of relief that you don't!)

Most of all, I hope this book serves as a gentle reminder to *all* of us to share our stories. They make us human. They help us connect. They really do matter.

Part I: Select Your Destination

Chapter 1: The Honeymoon ~ Somewhere in Time

1979 ~ Mackinac Island, Michigan

I felt . . .

What *did* I feel back then?

Young and in love, yes. But not *too* young. I chafed when anyone suggested that. We weren't babies. I mean, I was twenty-one and Rice, twenty-four.

Looking over at him, there behind the wheel of our Chevrolet Citation, I felt giddy. I basked in the warm breeze blowing in through the open window and found it fascinating to watch him drive. It wasn't, of course, but back then and there, I wanted to spend every minute I could with this man that I idealized and adored. My *husband*.

Did all newlyweds feel this way? This intense attraction, the desire to touch—all the time!—the constant rush of excitement and fascination. The hard part—the ceremony and reception—was behind us. As we began our married life together, I pictured us on a never-ending joyride filled with fun and carefree happiness. With occasional pit stops, of course.

One of our first pit stops occurred after a two-and-a-half-hour drive from Clare, Michigan, to the place where the fresh blue waters of two of the great lakes met (Huron and Michigan). We found parking, hauled our luggage to the ferry dock, then chose prime seats on the top deck and watched the sunlight sparkle off the water's surface. With a sigh, I leaned against Rice, breathing in the peaty lake air as the wind whipped through my hair. Ahhh, destination honeymoon was underway.

Less than twenty-four hours earlier, we'd tied the knot at Good Shephard Lutheran Church in Saginaw. The air had been pregnant with humidity, causing my hair to fall limp. My makeup ran before I even began the walk down the aisle on my stepbrother, Joe's, arm. I carried a bouquet of white daisies and baby's breath, not the dainty Queen Anne's lace I'd seen on the cover of a bridal magazine.

"Those things would die before you even reach the altar," the florist insisted.

So, I carried the sturdy daisies. From under my wide-brimmed lace hat, quite the rage after Farrah Fawcett wore one to marry Lee Majors, I peeked up the aisle toward Rice, who wore the sweetest smile—along with the most God-awful rental tux I'd ever seen. A white one.

I looked with longing at his groomsmen's handsome black tuxes. *Why in the hell had Rice chosen white?* For an instant, I wondered if he was having similar thoughts about my headgear. We didn't confer with each other on those kinds of things back then. Maybe some couples did, but not us. Nor did we write our own vows or consider a non-church service. And absolutely no way did we entertain the thought of seeing each other before the ceremony—we didn't need any bad luck if we were to have a long and happy marriage.

Memories from the ceremony and reception flash through my mind in snippets. Sun streaming through the glass windows near the altar as we said our vows. Our friends, Kaarin and Joel, singing a duet of Barbara Streisand's "Evergreen." Us, chugging cheap sparkling wine straight from the bottle as our best man and maid of honor drove us to the reception.

Upon arriving at the venue, a glitzed-up bowling alley, we found the reception area tucked out of sight from the lanes. We made an instant beeline for the mixed drink fountains. I think I had a vodka tonic, and Rice, maybe a seven-and-seven. After a sit-down dinner of chicken Kiev, a live band played big band and pop selections along with Midwestern classics like the polka, the hokey pokey, and the chicken dance. Our photographer (let's call him Zippy) trailed us so closely I thought he was trying to climb into my womb.

Several hours in, I was fried. Zippy wouldn't leave us alone, Rice's mom got physically ill from anxiety, and my hair was soaked, limp with perspiration under that damn hat. The party had reached the halfway mark. Maybe.

Sinking into a chair, I lit a cigarette. *Dammit.* What kind of bride smokes in her wedding gown? I mean, what would my friends' parents think? (Mind you, we were adults, as I already pointed out.) Thankfully, Zippy missed that *Princess Bride* moment when I slumped in the shadows, much like a wet rat, clenching a coffin nail between my parched lips.

But enough! The wedding chaos was over. We were on our honeymoon. Our freakin' honeymoon!

The lake water soothed me, lapping the rocky shoreline as we approached the pier. After the ferry docked, we shuffled along with the other tourists, lugging our bags, again soaked in sweat but this time smelling of tropical sunscreen. We ambled toward the main drag, where the scent of coconut gave way to that of fudge. And horse manure.

Mackinac Island has banned motor vehicles since it first became a popular summer resort in the 1890s. That's part of the charm, exploring the island's quaint shops and historic homes by foot, then renting a bike—or horses—to complete a loop of the 8.2-mile Lakeshore Boulevard around the island. Our own bike ride would have to wait until we found a place to stay, let alone store our luggage.

We dragged our bags, the clack of their wheels blending in with the energetic din of Main Street. Bicycles whizzed by. Children squealed, and horses snorted. I tried not to panic as "No Vacancy" signs accosted us every step of the way. See, we'd made no reservations. That's how we rolled back then.

Okay, we *had* reserved a room for our wedding night itself, when we'd driven to the Doherty Hotel in Clare, maybe an hour away from our reception. Friends had suggested we do that to get some distance from practical jokesters who might want to stick gauche "just married" signs on the back of our car . . . or tuck inflated condoms into the back seat.

Married friends predicted that we'd be hungry, and they were right. We hit a Burger King drive-thru on our way to Clare. Those same friends also said we'd be too wiped out to have sex.

"To hell with that," Rice said.

I'm pretty sure we *were* too tired, but we must have given it our best as the people in the next room knocked on the wall for us to keep the noise down. (Apologies to our adult children. I should have warned you to skip over that part.)

We did finally manage to score a room at the Mission Point Resort in Mackinac. Looking back, I'm thankful we found any lodging at all. Seems our honeymoon date overlapped with the annual 333-mile yacht race from Chicago to Mackinac Island. Bawdy sailing parties flanked the hotel's public areas, ready to celebrate whether they won, placed, or totally tanked in the race. Giddy to get to the sanctity of our own room, we jostled through the manic rush hour of mariners.

No one needed to worry about being too lusty or loud that night. No one.

While on Mackinac, we took part in some of the island's typical activities, like cycling around the island and making the steep climb up Arch Rock for a better view of glittering Lake Huron.

Before heading to the mainland, we hopped in a horse-drawn taxi to ride up the flower-lined street to the Grand Hotel. Against the din of the horses clopping up the hill, we visited with crew members who had just wrapped filming *Somewhere in Time* with Christopher Reeve and Jane Seymour. The movie wouldn't hit the theaters for at least another year. Of course, we would go to see it because, well . . . how could we not?

If I'm honest, I've never fully understood the film's storyline. Still, I've always enjoyed its opulent setting and beautiful stars, its early 1900s period costumes, and its haunting repeated threads from Rachmaninoff's *Rhapsody on a Theme of Paganini*. That song always takes me back . . . to the movie and the island . . . to our honeymoon . . . literally, to somewhere in time.

· ♥ ·

When our visit to Mackinac ended, we took the ferry back to the mainland and drove farther north, into a town called Paradise in Michigan's upper peninsula—fondly called the U.P. While we felt reticent to spend too much time or money on a honeymoon right before relocating to Colorado, we hadn't wanted to be outdone by friends who were cruising or visiting resorts in celebration of their own nuptials. On a lark, we picked Paradise for its name. And again, we made no reservations.

But wonders never cease. Curley's Motel had vacancies.

In Paradise, we saw the Tahquamenon Falls and then rowed to a small island where we waded in icy rust-colored water. I loved that, but Rice preferred touring the Whitefish Point Lighthouse and the Great Lakes Shipwreck Museum. While I'd heard—and liked—Gordon Lightfoot's haunting song, "The Wreck of the Edmund Fitzgerald," it chilled me to learn it was based on truth and that twenty-nine men sank with the ship on a stormy night in November 1975.

On a lighter note, we found a local place to splurge on steaks that night, after an appetizer of cheese and Ritz crackers accompanied by the peskiest, most persistent fly ever. That damned thing may still be living for all we know. Curley's is. An internet check confirmed it. And while I can't be certain, it may even have the same furnishings as it did back in 1979.

If parts of this honeymoon trip make us sound a bit lacking in class, what can I say? At times, we are. For sure, we were more than just a wee bit clueless back then. The wedding and honeymoon trip were, much like our life, a bit of a dramedy. Even a comedy of errors.

But I'll bet you're wondering, if this were an actual travelogue, would I recommend you make the same stops we did?

Mackinac Island, definitely. It remains a treasure, in my own heart and mind, but also to visitors from around the world. Rice and I have re-visited several times through the years. We've enjoyed riding the ferry with our kids and hearing them marvel as we've sailed across the Straits of Mackinac. ("It's like a mini ocean!") They've let us tag—or is that lag?— along as they've bicycled past each other, racing around the island. I even sympathized rather than scolded on the occasion they overdosed on the island's specialty, fudge. (Granted, I could have lived without the confession from one: "I ate so much of it, my poop turned green.")

Even given the possibility of colorful poop, I'd highly recommend a visit to the island.

As for an overnight stay in Paradise? I'll say this:

The town is a nature haven, and Curley's itself didn't seem so bad, back when we first came upon it. I mean, it had vacant rooms *and* free parking. Plus, it overlooked Whitefish Bay on Lake Superior, which it still does.

Then again, we may have been so young and crazy in love that it made us blind to some details.

A recent online review for Curly's complained about their room's musty odors, old carpet, and cheap polyester bedding. Had it always been that way? Or did we just overlook those things back when our hormones raced at a speed that would likely cause us bodily harm today?

Oh, yeah. Once upon a time, our world overflowed with possibilities. Little did we realize then that falling in love and lust was the easy part. We hadn't a clue that the true challenge would be to create enough luck together to *stay* in love.

So far, knock on wood, we've been lucky. While we may not be young, Rice and I still have the love and crazy parts going for us. But are those enough to lure us back to Curley's?

I confess, our memories of Paradise still bring a smile. Yet we've come to enjoy our creature comforts. So, it's not on our bucket list to return to Curley's anytime soon. At least not in this lifetime.

But we still look back on the free parking fondly.

· ♥ ·

Revisiting memories made and lessons learned thus far:

- Favorite wrong turn: I forgot to pack a bra for the honeymoon. Oops.

- Travel tip gleaned: Pack light, but not in the underwear department.

- Insight into marriage: Never forget, paradise is a state of mind.

Chapter 2: The Newlywed Blues ~ Year One Was Not That Fun

1980 ~ Iowa, Nebraska, Colorado

S o, why Colorado? The best answer I have is: Why not?

After two winters as a Central Michigan University grad student, Rice was ready to leave Michigan's gray skies behind. Personally, I loved my state, all crystal white and crisp in winter, a mix of aqua and sand-colored waterscapes come warmer weather. And fall ushered in the scent of pine, wafting through maples and oaks that glimmered in patches of orange, red, and gold.

That said, the world awaited. I felt all grown up and ready to live somewhere new.

Neither of us knew what or where we wanted to be when we grew up. While student teaching, I learned I didn't like life in the classroom from the other side of the desk. When Rice said he might like to continue with more grad school, I was all in.

He narrowed his choices to three doctoral programs in speech communication—the University of Florida in Gainesville, the University of Arizona in Tucson, and the University of Colorado in Boulder.

In the end, we chose Colorado.

• ♥ •

Occasionally, in my mind's eye, I catch a glimpse of our dog, Sam—sandy-haired, shaggy, and stoned—riding shotgun with Rice up front in a U-Haul truck as we headed west toward Colorado. We thought we were doing the right thing, medicating Sam for the trip.

Our cat, Harry, would have none of that nonsense. He rode with me, skittering about the back seat of our navy Citation, undrugged, yowling at will, and pooping in the house plants a time or two because—well, what is a traveling cat supposed to do?

It's not saying much, but I liked road trips much more than our pets did. For one thing, we, as humans, could learn a bit about each state as we passed through. Iowa, for example, is famous for its pork tenderloins, loose-meat sandwiches, and corn, lots and lots of corn. Rice, stuck with a limited radio station selection in the U-Haul, recalls listening to a local call-in show that discussed those specialties, as well as soybeans and Snickers salad. Plus, eggs.

"If I never hear another thing about eggs . . ." he's been known to still say.

Iowa's farmlands stretched out before us in small, gentle hills. Soybean leaves and corn tassels glittered in the sun. Millions of pink and purple wildflowers danced in the median, showing off their colors for miles along Interstate 80.

At first, Nebraska brought more lush farmlands. Then fields spiked with goldenrod gave way to a more desert-like landscape of vast, stark plains interrupted by occasional bluffs.

At the Nebraska-Colorado state line, a sign read, "Welcome to Colorful Colorado." Rice and I both honked our horns on seeing it, a goofy, giddy travel tradition we continue to this day. I glanced all around, seeking the colorful sights the sign promised, but the joke was on me. Myriad browns and tans and ochres flanked the highway.

An occasional tumbleweed bounced across the lonesome road. Harry's skittish yowls kept me from dozing off as we followed the bland terrain into the dark. After what seemed like forever, we pulled up in front of our new rental house in the pitch of night with a sedated dog and a pissed off cat. Too exhausted to make a pallet for sleep, we sacked out on the floor.

Colorful Colorado, my ass. But this was now home.

· ♥ ·

The CU-Boulder campus bustled with winding walkways and red-tiled buildings tucked into the rustic Flatiron Mountains. Colorado was hot but not humid. The higher altitude winded us, but we handled the jaunt up University Hill just fine. We enjoyed the Hill's eclectic shops and bars and, at a place called the Sink, we discovered a culinary marvel we enjoy to this day when the server brought honey along with our pizza.

"Drizzle this on any leftover crust," he said, "and voila, you've got dessert too."

Not too far from campus, downtown Boulder beckoned, its quaint pedestrian mall lined with more diverse shops and pubs and eclectic energy. We caught delicious whiffs from the Falafel King and then Mrs. Fields' Cookies while we strolled past musicians and street entertainers in action. My favorite was Evan from Heaven, who walked a slack rope he installed between light posts, using only his body and arms to find balance.

A few blocks over, we found *the* house on Pine Street, Mork and Mindy's place from the hit sitcom of the same name. In the show's opening, the stars fly a kite in Chataqua Park, its meadows bordered by blue skies and purple mountains. Then Mork, wearing a blue-and-orange striped shirt with rainbow suspenders, hands Mindy a tiny but perfect wildflower he's picked.

Magic like that led us to Boulder. But its cost-of-living plunked us down sixteen miles north, in a hamlet called Longmont, more of a family community than a university town.

My 100-words-per-minute typing skills landed me a job as an executive secretary at AMF Head, a job I sucked at. My degree in business education was wasted, working for the VP of Finance, a man who made sure I knew my priorities: to keep the coffee hot and plenty and to go to the vending machine for his snacks, more times a day than I care to remember. Eventually, I passed shorthand notes back and forth with the other executive secretary (excuse me, the SENIOR executive secretary) about what an a-hole he was. That first day, though, I behaved myself and tried to get a sense of the job. I was the breadwinner, after all.

Rice started to work on his Ph.D. in communication but soon discovered he wasn't enamored with CU's program. It took him some time to figure out why—and to admit it to me. His previous work in communication programs had always focused on debate and forensics. At CU, no one else had that background. "I just want to be a debate coach," he told me eventually. "I didn't realize there was all this other crap involved."

Dear God, what had we done? We were broke, I was lonely and hated my job, and my happy-go-lucky Rice was struggling too.

For my birthday in October, he bought me a floral arrangement from Safeway—a faux tabletop tree stump with fabric flowers sprouting from its center. I cried softly in bed that night at his sweet yet pathetic gift . . . and because I felt like a bitch to react to it like such a baby. As Christmas approached, I told Rice I needed a Michigan fix. We drove back to visit family and party with newlywed friends, who had honeymooned in *real* paradise places and then returned home to their roots. *My* roots. They seemed so happy. I wanted that. To be happy.

With the new year, I can't say that Rice and I became suddenly happy, but we did resolve to try to dive into more Colorado-centric activities. I'd grown up skiing—granted, not well—and now I worked for a company that doled out free passes and loaner ski packages. So, when two other couples who also had passes invited us to hit the slopes with them, we jumped on the chance.

The drive to Winter Park opened my eyes to a new side of Colorado, the Western Slope. We traversed Berthoud Pass, trying not to fret about signs that warned us to *Watch for Falling Rock* or the one that pointed the way to a *Runaway Truck Ramp*. We'd worry about those things later, if need be. Instead, we focused on crossing the majestic Continental Divide.

Skipping by Winter Park's epicenter, we headed straight to the slopes. Rice had skied once before, and badly. No worries. One of the other couples also hailed from the Midwest, and that helpful we've-got-this pride shone through. Rice didn't need no stinkin' lessons. He had us.

His challenges began right away with a thing called the snowplough, or wedge, a common beginner's technique for stopping. It requires the skier to point the front tips of the skis together while spreading the back of the skies wider and forming a triangle, or wedge, with them.

"You're not doing it," I scolded Rice.

"I'm trying!" he insisted.

He hopped on the chairlift just fine, and we started our ride without any tangled scarves or dropped ski poles. As we approached the hilltop, I coached him to lean over his skis, stand when they touched the ground, and let the chair glide him forward, out of the way.

I demonstrated what I'd told him, certain that he would follow my lead. Yet the next thing I knew, the chairlift stopped, and its boundary fence collapsed. Rice had taken it out. Unintentionally, of course. But still.

"It was awesome," he told me later, "hearing my wife's cackling laughter echo off the mountains while strangers helped me get back on my skis."

He wasn't back on his skis for long before he fell again. But this time, he couldn't get up. "What did you expect?" he said. "You all were asking me to ski over moguls."

I'm not so sure about that, but I can't argue with his next assessment.

"I'm never going to get it. My knees want to go downhill, but my upper body doesn't."

Members of the National Ski Patrol came to assist, hauling a makeshift ambulance sled. They used it to tow Rice back down to the lodge, which is the next place I saw him, sitting near the fire with his leg outstretched in a makeshift cardboard contraption to protect his knee.

"Are you okay?" I asked, hopeful he wasn't in pain.

"I'm good." His face glowed. "The Ski Patrol took me down the hill slowly and told me to catch some rays and enjoy the ride. So, I did."

He looked happy. Jovial even. I hadn't yet realized that his glow was not from the skiing but from the fact he was several toddies in.

The next day, he suggested, "Why don't we go out for breakfast?"

"Okay," I agreed. "Anywhere special?"

"Somewhere near the hospital," he replied. "Then we can head to the ER afterward."

I wasn't so sure his injury merited an emergency room visit. But, hey, I was among the fools who took him out to ski on moguls before he was ready. He wasn't about to accept my judgment again.

At the ER, sometime mid-morning on a thankfully slow Sunday, a nurse led Rice back to the exam room.

"Would you mind if some interns observe?" the attending doctor asked.

Rice agreed. I cringed as I watched several student doctors manhandle his knee, and then again when I heard the attending mutter words like "torn fibers" and "the meniscus."

When he finished the exam, he turned to the interns. "You'll see this a lot." He pointed to Rice's knee. "It's a very common ski injury."

Then he ordered Rice some crutches to use for a couple weeks, followed by walking and maybe some bicycling to regain strength in his knee.

That's it? I wanted to say.

But I let Rice have the last word, and as we left the hospital, he muttered, "I am never skiing again in my life!"

Just like that, with one mournful twist of the Riceman's knee, our winter of free fun on the Colorado slopes ended.

· ♥ ·

Around that time, Rice got a job selling cars on top of going to school to help ends meet. He worked six days a week, which made me even more miserable. Here we were, living in this beautiful place but with little time or money to enjoy it.

Meanwhile, out-of-state visitors flocked to visit us. Friends who had money to ski . . . and to eat at places we couldn't afford, sometimes on fancy expense accounts. My misery became more bitter than I care to admit, and I told Rice I wanted to try living somewhere more affordable. That was my coping tool back then, running away. Toward what? Didn't matter. Toward something, anything, new and different.

"Where do you want to go?" he asked, stupefied.

"Madison, Wisconsin, sounds nice. Like Boulder, but back in the Midwest."

He said nothing, and I read his silence as assent. The next day I made a downpayment on a U-Haul rental. In my mind, we would be Madison-bound come June.

As March became April, local parks grew green and lush with wildflowers popping up everywhere. Thousands of tulips bloomed on the Pearl Street Mall alone, and the scent of Colorado blue spruce and pine made way for the pungent addition of freshly cut grass.

Rice and I had bought bikes with our wedding money but had yet to ride them.

Or so I thought. Until I was paying bills one Sunday morning and found an invoice from the hospital ER.

"What in *the* hell is this?" I asked, waving it in my husband's face.

He reached out to steady the sheet so he could read it. "Ah," he said. "Remember how the ER doc told me to ride my bike to strengthen my knee after my fall on the ski slopes?"

"Yeah?"

"Well, I was doing just that when I flew over my handlebars trying to stop."

My eyes widened. "What?!"

"Sorry I forgot to tell you," he murmured. Then he perked up. "But on the upside, the doc was impressed I was doing PT on the bike."

"Wait a minute . . . You saw the same doctor after both falls?"

"Yeah." Rice shot me a sheepish grin. "He said I just bruised my shoulder. But he warned me not to forget my bike has hand brakes, not foot brakes, the next time I take it out."

That spring brought other surprises too. I found a new job, teaching office skills to adults through the Job Training Partnership Act. I worked with a woman named Helen, who, along with her husband, Hugh, took Rice and me underwing and got us on the road to growing up together.

I still cried a lot. Growing up is hard, you know. But around the same time that I changed jobs, so did Rice. Again. And we suddenly had something we hadn't had before. Two-day weekends.

Our reservations for the Madison-bound U-Haul came and went. I didn't notice until several months had passed. Seems that happiness, while still evasive, was starting to bud.

We dined out more, often with Helen and Hugh, who frequently treated.

"Pay it forward someday," they said when we objected. And we've tried to do just that.

Many of our favorite restaurants have since closed, like Pearl's and Potters on the mall and the James, which served Irish pub fare and good hearty beer. Sebanton in Longmont, which served authentic French food and the best chocolate cheesecake I've ever tasted. It seems that restaurants, much like people and relationships, have seasons to grow and seasons to die.

As far as travel, we did a whole lot of Colorado to Illinois to Michigan and back trips. I still missed family and friends badly, and the price to visit—free!—was right.

Never mind that we still both worked a fifty-week year. We were making progress.

Our new home was starting to live up to its name—Colorful Colorado.

· ♥ ·

Revisiting memories made and lessons learned thus far:

- Favorite wrong turn: It took a long while—until 2023—to get to Madison, Wisconsin.

- Travel tip gleaned: Traveling outside our comfort zone teaches us who we really are.

- Insight into marriage: Don't be a cheap fool; pay a stranger for ski lessons.

Chapter 3: Growing as Two ~ Getting the Hang of Marriage

Early 1980s ~ Denver, Estes Park, More Colorado Mountain Country

On our first Memorial Day, we drove up to Estes Park and followed Trail Ridge Road into the Rocky Mountain National Park. The highest paved road in the U.S. park system, Trail Ridge wound past one natural wonder after another, including the clear blue waters of Bear Lake.

"Ooooh." I squealed. "Can we come back here some time in summer to swim?"

"Not unless you want to die of hypothermia," Rice replied.

Right. We weren't in Michigan anymore.

I had to admit, though, Colorado's snow *was* more magical than Michigan's. When Boulder's winter skies darkened and a cold front rolled in, snow followed, sometimes a dusting, more often a dump load. Once the clouds cleared, the sky became a blue canvas, a backdrop to patches of gray and purple and white mountains in the distance. Then a chinook would blow through—a dry, warm wind, blasting at up to 80 miles per hour—and the snow would evaporate.

I turned my attention from Bear Lake to the elk grazing the meadows, their noses nuzzling the grasses that rustled in the wind. At the next overlook, birds and insects chirped, and children chased marmots scurrying along rocks near the path's edge. As the Citation inched along the curved road, the terrain and climate changed from rocky crags butting against pine forests to a place too cold for trees to survive—a real-life tundra. I posed by a monstrous mound of ice, shivering in my sundress and sandals, an outfit just right for the 80-degree Boulder weather. But not for the much higher altitude of Estes Park in May.

Boulder's eclectic ways—it's live-and-let-live attitude—continued to fascinate us. Twice we went out to eat and found ourselves seated near couples reciting their own poetry to each other. One night, we watched a three-year-old girl in the booth across from us lift her mother's top to nurse after dinner. Speaking of breasts, we inched alongside two boobs (two men dressed as a pair of bosoms) during a Halloween crawl on the Pearl Street Mall. And we sneaked in looky-loo drives by Coot Lake, a nude beach near the IBM plant near our home between Boulder and Niwot. (Note to hopeful travelers: The city long ago shut the site down.)

One summer day, we followed State Highway 119 to visit the one-time mining towns of Black Hawk and Central City. We ventured into an old-time saloon, the Glory Hole, for burgers and beers. When we left the restaurant, we discovered it had sleeted during lunch. Lots and lots of sleet. We walked back to our car through a winter wonderland, right in the middle of summer.

In addition to adopting Boulder's live-and-let-live philosophy, we also embraced the let's-get-physical vibe all around us. We decided—*again*, but this time in summer—that we really needed to take advantage of our environment.

And, as Rice pointed out, "We need to attempt to find hobbies we can enjoy together. Adult-type hobbies. Things besides going to college bars."

We started hiking, checking out several short trails that were near to Boulder. These treks filled our hearts (and lungs) with Boulder's beauty and a taste for its healthy lifestyle. Our interest piqued when we noticed folks carrying backpacks and veering off path just a tad to break ground and set up camp. Eventually, we, too, invested in some camping gear. Not REI-style camping equipment; surplus Army-Navy stuff better suited our style.

Geared with backpacks and Sterno stoves, freeze-dried meals and water-purification tablets, we traversed the foothills' switchbacks, proud to venture into a space where no public campsites could be had.

I'm not sure how long we hiked before we started to snipe at one another. Rice liked to move at a clipped pace, whereas I often stopped to hug a tree, catch my breath, and holler for him to slow the hell down. After what felt like quite some time, we came to a small glassy lake.

"This would be a great place to make camp," I suggested.

"Let's go just a bit further," he countered.

Biting back irritation, I followed him for another half hour or so. He stopped abruptly.

"Sonofabitch." His words came out in a soft, hissing whisper.

My heart pounded as I peeked around him, hoping we hadn't encountered a snake. We hadn't. We'd just hiked so far we'd reached another public road, with an adjacent parking lot. Irked—each of us for different reasons, of course—we backtracked to the lake, set up camp, and got over ourselves enough to enjoy the rest of the journey—notwithstanding our bland, re-hydrated astronaut meals.

Later that summer, another couple invited us camping, suggesting we meet up past Ward, make camp near where we parked, then venture out on day hikes into the canyons.

"Sounds great," I said, happy to hear a plan that allowed for coolers of real food, not freeze-dried astronaut packets. A modern outhouse nearby with a small sink. And toilet paper.

As Rice steered the Citation up the road past Ward, the terrain grew rocky. My breathing quickened. "Let's turn back," I said.

"We'll be fine," he assured me.

Fine schmine. We'd just spent a chunk of change on new tires, after buying our first house, a cute yellow ranch in a subdivision called Gunbarrel Estates. We weren't dirt poor, but we weren't flush. I hated to fret about money, but I did. Mature as I was, I climbed into the back seat, grabbed a beer from the cooler, and rode the rest of the way, sulking on the floor.

Rice was right, though. We made it to our destination just fine, met up with Chris and Carla, pitched our tents, and had a relaxing evening.

The real fun began the next morning.

Rice didn't smile as he greeted me on his return from his morning constitutional. "I hate to tell you this, honey, but your contacts fell down the hole in the john."

What was he saying? I'd tucked my contact lens case into his Dopp kit.

"Why would you take your Dopp kit into the outhouse?" I tried to keep a steady tone.

"To brush my teeth."

Ewww. Granted, the outhouse had a sink. Still, I shivered, trying not to think about it.

Rice continued. "I went to set the kit on the ledge near the latrine. But you never zipped the kit closed." He paused. "And somehow your case fell out of it."

I inhaled sharply, no longer fixated on the gross factor. My mind's eye saw dollar bills floating about me like dust in the wind—which was ironic because, if dollar bills floated by me like dust in the wind, my real eyes wouldn't be able to see them because my contacts were in the shitter. My gosh-darned hard contact lenses, the ones that made me feel like a nail was gouging my eyeball when a speck of dust got in them . . . I purchased those babies once a year, a single pair costing several hundred dollars. And they were gone?

Now I'd have to wear my ugly Coke-bottle-lensed glasses for the unforeseeable future.

"Don't cry, honey." Rice looked like he might want to cry too. Or maybe what I saw in his eyes was fear. Fear that I might start to cuss or stomp my feet or call him names, right there in front of Carla and Chris.

For a moment, the crisp mountain air cocooned us in silence.

Then God bless Chris. He punched Rice's arm in a good-buddy gesture. "I'll bet we can get that case back," he wagered.

Carla and I watched—from a slight distance—as they rigged a fishing line, gobbed it with chewing gum on the end, and cast it down the hole, trying to get my case to stick to it. No dice. Oh, the fishing line worked, but the guys needed something besides gum to grasp the case.

Chris grabbed an empty soda can and cut it open, making a scoop. And I kid you not. It worked! They retrieved my case and tucked it into a used sandwich bag for safe transport.

Trust me. I boiled the hell out of that case after we got back home. I threw out the pan I boiled it in too. But darned if those lenses didn't work just fine until next year's budget allowed me to buy new ones.

Frankly, I'm somewhat embarrassed to share this story. But as Rice pointed out, "How could you not share a shit show as awesome as this?"

· ♥ ·

Life continued to get better—at home, at work, *and* at play. Our careers merged onto a smoother track. Rice was recruited into an IT training program. I found a marketing job at a consulting firm a mile and a half from home. We started to feel more like grown-ups. Sort of.

Our mode and style of travel also improved. In Vail, we canoodled in the Westin's hot tub, blanketed in steam as the snow kissed our cheeks and eyelashes. We celebrated our birthdays at the Brown Palace in Denver, opting for cocktails in lieu of the hotel's iconic afternoon tea. And we returned to Estes Park, to our first Bed & Breakfast, the delightful Riversong, where we soaked in a clawfoot tub before sipping wine in front of a crackling fire.

For the health of it, we joined the Cottonwood Athletic Club, a small place in Niwot where I attended an exercise class clad in Jane Fonda leggings while Rice lifted weights and enjoyed the hot tub and sauna. We started running and entered one of the earliest Bolder Boulders, a Memorial Day race that's been labeled *America's Best All-Time 10K*.

"Start out slow," Rice cautioned as we lined up at the back of the pack.

At the one-mile mark, on passing the time clock, his eyes widened.

"We need to pick up our pace," he said, and I stumbled to match his widening stride.

"I don't think a thirteen-minute mile was *that* bad," I tell him today, as we reminisce together.

"Jan." His silvery eyebrows arch, and his blue eyes flash. "It was a seventeen-minute mile."

I stand by my original thirteen-minute claim. But I will take credit for slowing our pace to savor the experiences along the way. Live bands performed as we passed belly dancers and bagpipers and people dressed like apes—or Elvis! Even at our lowly pace, trotting barely in front of the EMT's caboose, the crowd still thundered applause when we crossed the finish line.

As I've said, life was good. We were finding our stride—at home, at work, at play.

And then I got baby fever.

· ❤ ·

Revisiting memories made and lessons learned thus far:

- Favorite wrong turn: Visiting restaurants on open poetry night. Believe it or not, I kind of miss that.

- Travel tip gleaned: Remember, mishaps often become the best of adventure stories.

- Insight into marriage: Hold off on thoughts of divorce (or homicide) when you have PMS or the flu . . . or when you've just watched the hubs fish for treasures from the pit latrine of an outhouse, no matter how modern.

Chapter 4: Add a Kid to the Mix ~ And Everything Becomes a Crapshoot

Mid-1980s ~ Hawaii, Cancun, Playa del Carmen ~ Mexico; Key West ~ Florida

I worked up until the day I delivered a stubbornly breech-positioned baby by C-section. After a twelve-hour labor, I was too foggy to enjoy the most exciting part of the birthing journey—something I learned about later that has become legend in the annals of family stories.

"Everything moved at lightning speed," Rice still recalls. "I'd just returned from the drug store." He'd gone to pick up a disposable camera. "The minute I got back, the nurse tossed me a gown and gloves as they wheeled you away to prep for an emergency C-section."

My eyes twinkle, knowing what's next. "And she promised to come back for you after—"

"All right, all right." He cuts me off, but he can barely hide an indignant grin. "I could have sworn she told me to strip down before I put on the gown."

Rice participated in the birth, his tighty-whities-clad ass peeking from the backside of his hospital-issued gown as he cut the umbilical cord.

After a five-day hospital stay (standard for C-sections back in 1984), we loaded our infant girl, Alex, into the Citation for the drive home, and my husband became a responsible old man overnight. At least he drove like one. Me? I became a contortionist, gawking from the passenger seat to ensure that Alex, slouched in a massive car seat behind me, continued to breathe.

The next day, Mother's Day, we dropped our baby girl off in the church nursery. The attendant furrowed her brow. "She's so tiny." *Of course, she's tiny*, I thought. She's an infant. Now I confess, before that day, I'd never paid much attention to babies in church. After that day, I noticed that most new moms kept their babe in a carrier seat on the pew next to them. For several months following the birth.

I also missed the memo on how long to wait before taking a newborn out into the world. I felt good and wasn't ready to grasp how having a baby might change our lifestyle. Rice still ribs me about the luxury home tour of Vail my mom scheduled for all of us on his first Father's Day. I'm sure one-month-old Alex enjoyed it more than he did, even if she never cracked a smile. (I know, I know, a baby's first social smile doesn't appear before six to eight weeks. I *did* get that memo.)

When I returned to work, six weeks postpartum, my sister Lisa spent her summer break as our nanny. At lunchtime I drove home to nurse and burp my baby, after which "Billie Jean" blared from the boom box while we danced. Thanks to Michael Jackson and Lisa—and privilege I didn't realize I had—we made it through my return to work without major hiccups.

Summer ended and Lisa returned to college. Alex adjusted to daycare just fine, but I began to feel a disconnect with my work. I was the only one of three young and hungry management consultants who wasn't single and childless. The other two didn't mind pulling together proposals on nights and weekends, and they jumped at opportunities to travel. A local consultant was not an expert, or so the old joke went.

My first post-baby consulting gig took me to Dallas. I forgot to pack a hairbrush, only discovering it the morning I prepared to meet my new client. *Shit, shit, shit.* No worries, though. I brushed my teeth, then styled my hair with a blow dryer and the toothbrush. At the time, I thought my hair turned out okay, but looking back, my client *might* have spent an uncomfortable amount of time looking at me, and not in a way that sends the message, "Man, you look good."

A bit after Alex turned one, Rice and I took her to visit my sister Lynne and her family near Atlanta. We toted baby essentials up the wazoo, requested bulkhead seating, and boarded the plane early. We even brought a bottle to give to Alex when we ascended, to protect her ears from popping. Weren't we the savvy family travelers?

Why, yes. Yes, we were.

Until the blowout. By the child, not the plane.

There's nothing quite like trying to be discreet as people walk past you, sniffing the air as a frown crept over their faces. Unless it's squeezing a semi-claustrophobic adult, a wriggling, messy baby, and a diaper bag into an airplane lavatory. Of course, that couldn't happen until the line for the tiny lavatory eased up. And then, to add delight to an already lovely situation, turbulence hit amid changing Alex, and the contents of her diaper bag spilled all over the place.

Oh, yeah. Houston, we have a problem.

On the upside, upon arrival, we enjoyed Georgia's early summer lushness and visits to Grant Park, Cyclorama, and the zoo. Best of all, we lounged by the neighborhood pool for hours, just steps away from Lynne's house. I left Georgia just a bit envious of what I perceived to be a more relaxed lifestyle.

Back in Colorado, Rice's work picked up. He oversaw the Honeywell end of his firm's conversion to IBM. Ensuring that projects remained intact while the conversion happened involved some overnights at the office. This went on for weeks. One of his co-workers said his wife showed her kids a picture and said, "Don't forget this guy. His name is Daddy."

Miffed even after it ended, I still contemplated sending Rice's resumes out without his knowledge. I dreaded phone calls at night or on weekends. A work glitch meant a forty-five-minute drive into Denver. This was, after all, pre-iPhones and teleworking. Before laptops.

During one after-dinner call, Rice's posture stiffened. "My boss," he mouthed to me, covering the receiver with his hand. Teeth clenched, I left the room, not wanting to hear, or worse, cause a scene. When Rice got off the phone, he joined me, his expression hard to read.

"What does he want now? Your blood?" My temples throbbed, threatening to explode.

"Actually, no." A smile was starting to tug at Rice's lips. "He just wanted to say, as a bonus for all my hard work, he'd like to send us on a paid trip to Hawaii."

· ♥ ·

We left Alex with my sister Lisa (who flew in to babysit) and, after a crazy long flight, we began our stay in Hawaii on Honolulu's Waikiki Strip. I'd been there before—in high school with my family on vacation. My stepdad traveled there for work, and we got to tag along, so I'd already sailed on a dinner cruise at sunset, visited the Dole Pineapple Plantation, and toured the USS Arizona at Pearl Harbor.

Rice had done none of those things, but he only cared about that last one, so he boarded a bus, solo, ready to drink in the history at Pearl Harbor. Meanwhile, I lathered myself with a tropical-scented suntan lotion, breathed in the sea salt while sipping pre-made Mai Tais from the ABC Store, and dipped my toes in the ocean. Ahhh.

While I already suspected I'd had a better day than Rice, he confirmed as much that night at dinner.

"An hour into the bus ride," he said, "I discovered I was on the wrong bus."

"Oh, no."

"Yes. I had to backtrack and re-do the entire trip."

"But you did get to see Pearl Harbor?" I was watching a young Japanese couple at a nearby table nearby. The wife poured her husband's drink and waited for him to eat first.

Rice nodded. "It was a great day." Noticing the couple, he added, "That's nice, isn't it?"

Maybe I bristled because he quickly added, "I'm not hinting for you to do likewise. I just appreciate experiencing different places and people and their cultures."

It's true. I've always loved that about Rice, the way he savors history and drinks up all he can when it comes to different societies and customs. Suddenly, I felt shallow that I'd opted for Mai Tais on the beach rather than a re-visit to the USS Arizona.

To redeem myself—in my mind, not his—I suggested we visit the Polynesian Cultural Center (PCC) together the next day. I had read it's like Walt Disneyworld's Epcot, with little Polynesian villages inviting visitors to experience the food, art, jewelry, and handiwork of communities modeled after Samoa, Fiji, Tahiti, the Hawaiian Island Village. And more.

When we got off the bus at the Center and neared the entrance, Rice peered at the sign.

He turned to me. "I don't want to do this," he said softly.

"What?" I balked. "Why not?"

"It's run by a cult I don't care to support."

"You're kidding." I stared at him for a beat, then huffed back onto the bus, afraid to voice my anger and frustration lest I make a scene.

Years later, while reliving this trip together, Rice explained. "I didn't realize the Center is owned by the Church for Latter Day Saints. Our pastor back then always called the LDS a cult." He furrowed his brow. "I'm sorry I let that cloud my decision. I wish we had visited."

While Oahu provided moments of beauty and self-awareness, we liked Hawaii's big island better. We strolled quaint downtown Kona, past kiosks brimming with coconut-scented soaps and storefronts that displayed colorful clothing, stone jewelry, and hand-carved wooden art. Mahi-mahi and eggs for breakfast? Yes, please—along with getting a taste of *kālua puaʻa* (kālua pig) and poi while experiencing Polynesian music and dance at a traditional Hawaiian luau.

A highlight for me was taking a Captain Cook snorkel tour to Kealakekua Bay. Hawaiian spinner dolphins surfed the wake as our boat skimmed the pristine waters. Rice passed on the snorkeling, but I found it to be the perfect cool, wet break against the heat of the day. And the fish! Through my snorkel, I watched them dart about beneath the water's surface, a splendid variety including some oval-shaped yellow tang, slender gray-blue trumpet fish, and reef triggerfish in colorful geometric patterns.

On New Year's Eve Day, Rice drove our rented Suzuki along winding back roads up to Volcanoes National Park. We walked the stark landscape—black sand broken down from ropy remnants of previous lava flows. On the return drive, Rice slowed to avoid a teenage boy stooping in the middle of the road. As we neared, the boy ran off to the side of the road, and an explosion burst forth, the first of many firecrackers we'd experience to celebrate the incoming new year.

Back in the room, we had champagne while the fireworks danced on. To Rice's chagrin, I didn't make it up until midnight. Six-plus years into our marriage, I couldn't stay awake long enough to ring in the 1986 new year with my love in Kailua-Kona, Hawaii.

· ♥ ·

I *did* manage to make it till midnight the next new year—1987—during an extended family cruise to Cancun, Cozumel, and Key West. We arrived in Tampa the day prior to sailing to spend the night in a fancy hotel (now that's *my* kind of camping). Unfortunately, our ship quarters fell short.

Rice and I shared a three-bunk stateroom with Alex. Our cramped bathroom housed a commode and a stand-up shower as green as the cucumber-avocado soap I'd packed. I don't remember the name of the cruise line, but our ship was old, its amenities sparse. Meals were decent if not decadent. The cruise was Mom's gift to the family, and I could read disappointment in her eyes as she drank it all in. Our job boiled down to hiding any letdown of our own.

We dressed up each night for dinner but first met for cocktails and Bingo. Two-and-a-half-year-old Alex and her cousins, Erin (eight) and Andrea (nine), kicked major booty at this.

In Cancun, two cabs transported our group to a sister resort where we spent the afternoon. The cabbies drove beat-up vehicles in manic fashion to get us there. When one of the cabs broke down, the other driver pulled over, transferred a wire from beneath his cab to the other, and voila! Soon we were off again, leery until we arrived at a place with grass huts on the beach and a swim-up bar in the pool. We played hard and drank Coronas with lime, tipping the waiters lavishly. Or so we thought, until we realized we didn't know Jack about the exchange rates.

On New Year's Eve, we partied past midnight—I told you I could do it—dancing a conga line and drinking more champagne toasts than we should have. New Year's Day, we toured the Hemingway House on Key

West, entranced by its ropey old trees, Papa's massive desk, and all the six-toed cats. We had a great time—all except Rice.

"Perhaps he enjoyed himself a bit too much last night?" my mom suggested.

Indignant, Rice begged to differ. "I got dysentery," he insisted.

Dysentery? Who used that term in 1987?

Regardless, Rice blamed his delicate situation on the lettuce and tomato, which must have been washed before going on yesterday's burger out by the pool.

"I could barely take three steps outside the toilet," he recalls. "I had to go the doc, who gave me some sort of pill for it, and charged me $100 or something outrageous like that."

Needless to say, I have fonder memories of Key West than he does.

· ♥ ·

Revisiting memories made and lessons learned thus far:

- Favorite wrong turn: Learning that Rice stripped down to his skivvies to don his gown before Alex's birth. How I wish I'd been more alert to enjoy this.

- Travel tip gleaned: If you forget a hairbrush, call the front desk and ask for a comb.

- Insight into marriage: Learn to disagree with respect and a sense of fairness. As you improve, try this in public. (It's on our bucket list.)

Chapter 5: Traveling with Three Under Five ~ Oh, Hell to the No

Late 1980s ~ Colorado Springs; San Francisco, Sonoma ~ California

About the time Rice and I got the knack of traveling with one small child, our family expanded, starting when a second daughter, Quinn, arrived on the Fourth of July. But that's not all, folks. Eleven months later, on another holiday (Memorial Day), our son Daniel arrived, the first boy in either family in twenty-five years. Yes, he was a surprise! In a good way.

If you have babies close together like this, you'd best prepare for some ribbing. For example, at work, a co-worker waxed poetic about the challenges of parenting, first with just one child, then two, and then, in some cases, three or more. "Unless you're Jan." He smirked. "In her case, she might not have even noticed a difference between number two and number three?"

The funniest joke was not on us but on close friends we hadn't yet told that a third child was on the way.

"Mommy's gonna have a baby," Alex announced at a casual Sunday gathering.

"Oh, honey," our friend Pat corrected, "she already did."

"No." Alex let everyone know that she wasn't confused. "She's gonna have another one."

And the fun continued.

I've mentioned that traveling with one small child can seem like a crapshoot. I should add that traveling with three under five puts a whole new spin on the roulette wheel.

For one thing, we bought a tandem stroller just so we could leave the house. We also bought a second carrier, this one a backpack, so we could still hike as a family. On one such hike to St. Mary's Glacier near Idaho Springs, I felt a couple flash judging stares our way. Sure enough, I overheard the woman murmur to her partner, "You'd think they could wait to do this hike when the baby is a wee bit bigger."

She might have had a point. Yet you don't know what you don't know.

Re-evaluating some of our planned destinations through the eyes of a child, we rediscovered new spins on some old favorites. The Embassy Suites in Colorado Springs provided a great base for visits to Santa's North Pole and the Cheyenne Mountain Zoo. The kids loved the breakfast bar in the morning before heading out for our outing and lunch. We'd return for naps followed by the free happy hour with mocktails for the kids and cold ones for us.

When Alex mastered riding a two-wheeler, her dad and I decided to buy a trailer that he could tow behind his bike to transport the Dudes. Note: Quinn and Daniel were dubbed the Dudes once they seemed too old to be called babies. Not to brag, but this was before *The Big Lebowski* hit the theaters. *Our* Dudes were the originals (though they did anything but abide).

With an eye on our pennies, we scoured the want ads until we found a used bike trailer for sale. For years, we enjoyed that old Cannondale bugger, a two-wheeled trailer that connects to a bike's seat post. We'd bicycle as a family through our Gunbarrel Estates neighborhood, crossing a field that led to the Boulder Country Club. The ride wound along flat terrain and provided a killer view of Boulder's Flatirons. We also got to peek at some upscale houses. Then one day, our favorite field became a refugee village for displaced prairie dogs. Ah, Boulder.

Life was good. Except . . .

I found balancing work and family incredibly hard. I made career changes to ease my load. I transitioned first from consulting to teaching and then to doing data entry from home. Still, I struggled. I felt sad and inadequate.

What was I doing wrong?

If I asked that question today, someone might point out that my hormones were re-adjusting after having two babies so close together. Or maybe they'd just let me know that it's okay.

I don't remember how it came about—I suspect I was the instigator—but I ended up going to counseling to see if that would help.

"You're angry," a counselor told me at our first and only appointment. "Let's set up some biofeedback sessions to help you recognize and channel your feelings more appropriately."

What? I felt overwhelmed and exhausted, and she wanted to add to my calendar?

"I am *not* angry," I screamed, although not until I was out of her office, behind the wheel of Old Gray, the Taurus wagon we bought to replace the Citation.

Looking back, of course I was angry. It might have helped me more if she'd said that was perfectly normal. Moms my age—at least the privileged ones—were the first to have choices about our bodies, our relationships, our work. While I appreciated that, like I said, it was hard. If I worked, I felt like I should be at home. And vice versa.

Don't get me wrong. I chose to be a mom, all three times. But as one friend put it, "Being a mom is the most important job I've ever had. But I've never been more bored or frazzled."

Exactly. I was beyond frazzled, praying something – anything – would give.

Thankfully, something did.

Rice came home with news. He'd been selected to attend a work-related class in San Francisco. When my mom learned about it, she offered to travel from Michigan to watch the kids so I could go with him.

"Deal!" I said, before she could change her mind.

· ♥ ·

Rice's class took place at a hotel in South San Francisco in the Marina District. The property bordered the bay, and I sat near the water to bask in the breeze, reading, writing, and sketching—without interruption—while Rice attended classes.

"Don't you want to get out to explore on your own?" he asked when I met him for lunch.

"I'd rather do that with you." (Because I feared I'd get lost out on my own.)

So, starting that afternoon, after his classes, Rice drove us into the city, and like many others before us, we fell in love with San Francisco. We had a bucket list of things we wanted to see and do, like visit Fisherman's Wharf . . . eat Ghirardelli chocolate . . . and ride the ferry to Sausalito to walk on the waterfront and a gape at the houseboats.

We also wanted to ride the famous cable cars, which provided a great way to see the city. One of my favorite sites was the old painted ladies—ornate Victorian homes painted in three or more vibrant colors.

Late one afternoon, we hopped off a cable car in Chinatown. Vibrant red-and-gold banners streamed in its alleys, which smelled of baked goods and incense and ginseng tea. Shops overflowed with eclectic items for sale. Lots and lots of lucky cats and silk robes.

As we passed murals and temples and dim sum joints, I grew aware of the wall-to-wall people crowded around me, speaking fast in a language I couldn't understand. The subtle stench of urine grew stronger, and I realized this area was not just shops; it was also home to a huge population that lived here all jammed together—mostly elderly and, I suspect, impoverished.

I'm quite sure that Rice would have happily ordered food from a cart serving crispy fried duck and noodles right there in that alley. But I couldn't do it, not after taking in all the smells, getting caught in the bustle, and seeing whole Peking ducks and chickens, heads and feet intact, squished together and sitting out in the wet market ready for purchase. Instead, we ate at an Americanized Chinese restaurant where autographed photos of old movie stars decked the walls. I don't remember the food, only that the place felt inauthentic and staid. (So much for choosing a great dining experience in a city known for its classic restaurants.)

Another night, we went out for seafood somewhere along Fisherman's Wharf. Again, I don't remember the meal, but I do remember we dressed up. (My mom's new husband had hinted we might want to up our fashion game for the city.) Walking back to the car after dinner, a wild-eyed man jumped onto our path from behind a dumpster. I grabbed Rice's arm, certain my heart was about to jump from my chest. The man stared at us for what felt like forever. Then he yelled out some gibberish, turned away, and skittered off like a scared rat, as if *he* should be frightened of *us*.

We did our best to laugh off the night's big adventure on our drive back to the hotel. It had scared us, though—me, for sure, and I think Rice too. In fact, at one point I'd envisioned us being robbed, or worse, killed. Our babies would then become orphans, all because we had selfishly taken a break from them to explore the world.

By the next morning, my catastrophic thinking had ebbed, and I surprised myself by asking Rice a question: "Would you think I'm crazy if I said I'd like to explore Sonoma on my own today?"

His blue eyes flashed, and I waited for him to name some reasons it might be best if I didn't go off alone. Instead, with barely a pause, he looked me square in the eyes and said, "I take it you hear the call of the grape?"

God love him!

In truth, we both preferred beer over wine back then. If I opted for wine, I usually chose a sweet red, or even better, a white zin. Glen Ellen white zinfandel—in a box—was my hands-down favorite. Still, a ninety-minute road trip to wine country would make me feel sophisticated. And brave. I absolutely needed to make that trip, and Rice understood that.

But . . . have I mentioned my sense of direction?

Sad to say, I have no internal compass. And cell phones and GPS navigation systems had yet to be invented. Sure, there were maps, and I could read a map like an ace—*if* I was taking a test off a piece of paper. My troubles arose when it came to transferring information from a map to a three-dimensional cityscape. Shoot, even interstates could snag me at times. I once mistook Michigan's I-94 for I-96, ending up in Muskegon, not Kalamazoo, a cool 90-mile difference.

But past mishaps be damned. I got out of town just fine—past the Presidio, over the Golden Gate Bridge, then northbound to winding roads that passed orchards and family farms. Approaching Sonoma, I passed the Mission San Francisco Solano and the Sonoma barracks.

And then up ahead I saw it: Sebastiani Vineyard and Winery.

I parked and hustled into the hospitality center, where I joined a tour just getting started. A guide talked history and wine-making techniques while leading us through a room filled with redwood tanks. We passed through a spacious event center to get to my favorite spot, the tasting room. Sure, I'd had Sebastiani wine before. It was affordable enough (read: cheap) that we sometimes kept a big jug in the pantry back home. Still, here I was, taking part in an actual wine tasting all by myself in Sonoma Valley. How cool was that?

Back in the car, still pleased, I checked my clock and my map. I had time for one more winery, and I zeroed in on several marked on my map that were close to the Plaza.

I swear, I studied that map like a fiend. I really did. But, of course, I got lost.

Circling the plaza, I peered at the map at each stop, convinced I could sniff my way to a winery. I didn't care which one. As long as I didn't continue to pass the same boutiques and souvenir shops. Let me find something, please.

Gritting my teeth, I veered off the main drag and onto a tree-lined side road. I did it with absolute care and attention so I could find my way back to the Plaza if need be. However—hallelujah!—it led to a sign for a tasting room, and I followed a winding dirt road back to find it.

Believe it or not, the winery I found was Glen Ellen, home to my favorite white zin.

Looking back, while I loved and missed my kids, I also relished the sense of freedom I felt during this trip. My mom's stay with the kids had been such a gift. To Rice and me both.

It got me thinking.

If we lived closer to family, could we get away as a couple more often?

· ♥ ·

Revisiting memories made and lessons learned thus far:

- Favorite wrong turn: I didn't make one single bad turn getting back from Sonoma.

- Travel tip gleaned: Don't be afraid to use an old-fashioned map. Unless your name is Jan, in which case invest in the best kick-ass state-of-the-art navigation system you can afford.

- Insight into marriage (and family planning): For those who have heard that breastfeeding is an effective method of birth control: It isn't.

Part II: Prepare to Make a Detour

Chapter 6: Mama Needs Reinforcements ~ But What's With All This Humidity?

1991 ~ Georgia

Our couple's trip to California left me restless. I'd tasted the deliciousness of going on an outing without an entourage, thanks to family support. Also, I'd enjoyed being close to *real* water—not icy lakes that cause hypothermia or artificial reservoirs the size of postage stamps.

I had an itch to experience living somewhere new, somewhere that wasn't Michigan or Colorado. (Not California either, given the cost of living.) Rice didn't feel the same. He had fallen in love with Boulder.

He no longer commuted to Denver, having landed an IT position at a pharmaceutical company two miles from our house. Many days, he bicycled to work, came home for a sandwich at lunchtime, and then bicycled back to the office to finish his workday. In addition, he became involved with local politics. I enjoyed that vicariously through him. But heaven help us when he volunteered to work fundraising game nights. He'd come home reeking of cigarette smoke, and I could picture him proctoring a room full of older folks, hunched over the multiple cards laid out before them, eager to shriek out the first "Bingo!"

Rice loved Boulder now. *Everybody* loved Boulder. Well, almost everyone.

One time at church, during a casual discussion about the afterlife, someone joked, "How could heaven be better than this? I mean, we're in Boulder."

That elitist attitude stuck in my craw. More and more, I found Georgia on my mind.

When I dropped subtle hints about moving—e.g., "Did you know the cost of housing in Georgia runs 33% lower than it does here?"—Rice didn't bite. Not right away. What finally got his attention was this: We were outgrowing our house. Our sweet yellow ranch (which Alex named Timmy, by the way) had only three bedrooms, meaning the girls shared a room. Not devastating at the ages of two and six, but how would that fly when they were nine and thirteen?

Our family had already planned for a Georgia Christmas that year, so I decided to flat out ask Rice, "If I can line up a job interview for you during our visit, will you go for it?"

To my surprise, he agreed. He probably thought the odds were against me pulling it off. But I had previously done some executive search work, helping client firms find the right individual for professional positions. Using reverse tactics—plus a few of Rice's IT industry directories—I placed some calls to the Atlanta area, scoping out potential employers.

In December, we discovered the joy of driving cross country with three kids, ages six and under.

"Who farted?" Alex groaned, after we'd barely pulled out of the driveway.

Oh, yeah. That was the first sign that the fun was about to begin.

Being a seasoned mom, I packed enough food and drink to last each kid a month. Soon the fart reports got replaced with another chant.

"I gotta pee. Now!"

On one such call-of-nature stop, Quinn pointed at a woman mere feet away from us.

"Aww," she cooed, loud enough that I'm sure the lady heard. "A baby grandma!"

In her defense, Quinn was not yet three, and she absolutely loved all things miniature back then. (Come to think of it, she still does.) I wasn't embarrassed by her words or tone, both tinged with admiration. It was the way she kept oohing and cooing, all the while pointing at the elderly little person across the aisle.

Overall, we did okay on that trip. I didn't even snap right away, not until maybe the thirty-first time one of the girls complained, "Daniel is looking at me again!"

Our Georgia holiday ushered in lights and wonders that warmed my heart, already full from the charm of the Marietta Square with its unique shops, over-the-top decorations, and carolers singing our favorite songs. The kids bonded with aunts and uncles and cousins and indulged in too many Christmas cookies to mention.

And in between the gifts and the magic, Rice interviewed at Southern Company Services.

· ♥ ·

Back in Boulder post holidays, life got busy again. I'd almost forgotten about Rice's interview in Georgia. Then in April, he got an offer.

"The salary boost isn't substantial," he pointed out through our shell shock.

"True," I agreed. "But the cost of housing is so much more reasonable."

He nodded. "They'll pay for the move."

I raised my eyebrows. Was it worth it?

"Plus," he added, "they'll fly us down for a house-hunting trip. On their nickel."

We decided it was worth it.

Getting ready to sell the house created some challenges. Back then, I handled internal paint jobs myself, which was extra fun with a two- and a three-year old underfoot. I handed the little ones' brushes and buckets of water, praying they'd find that satisfying enough to leave the real Sherwin Williams alone. Thankfully, it worked.

Holding a garage sale provided another hurdle, but not to brag, may I say I did myself proud? I set up a great display of baby items and maternity clothes. I even packaged those old disposable "Kid Cuisine" plates, the kind with dividers for the different food groups, and sold them ten for a dollar. Rice was mortified I would do such a thing, but also a bit proud (I think). Heaven only knows, we went through a boatload of Kid Cuisines back in the day. And I sold out of those ten-for-a-dollar packages rather quickly.

More difficult than setting up for the sale was how to handle curious neighbors.

"Why are you getting rid of so much stuff? You moving or something?"

We hated to operate on the down-low, but one neighbor worked with Rice, and we didn't want to spill the beans about relocating in case the offer fell through.

I breathed with relief once Rice received employment clearance. On the day he planned to give notice, I kissed him good luck before work, giddy to ditch this top-secret life. He'd been gone twenty minutes at most when a call came into the house from Southern Company.

"Has Jim put in his resignation yet?" The HR rep sounded anxious.

My heart thundered against my chest. "I don't know. Is there a problem?"

"Just a small one. But we need to rescind his offer. Temporarily."

My fingers shook and I prayed Rice had not given notice as I called to share the news, something about a breach in the chain of custody while handing off Rice's urine sample for drug testing in transit. My disappointment was huge, but thankfully, he hadn't resigned yet. What else could we do but grin and jump through the hoops again?

Rice finally got cleared for employment again in late May, and this time it stuck. We flew down to Georgia to look for a house in early June. I basked in the weather, sunny with low humidity, and I drooled at the wide selection of homes in our price range. Even new builds came completely landscaped. I'm sure our realtor got sick of how much I insisted on a lot with mature trees—near good schools. She stuck with us, though. When we made an offer on a Leave-it-to-Beaver house in a cul-de-sac right by the neighborhood pool, it went through without a hitch.

In late June, Rice moved in with my sister Lynne and her family in Powder Springs so he could report to his new job in Atlanta. I stayed behind with the kids to sell our house in Boulder.

It sold in three days. Thank God. Because the real fun had not yet begun.

The buyer's home inspector turned up leaky showers to fix and double-paned windows to replace. We weren't surprised. Then came the radon specialist, who politely dodged the kids as they ran around the house, still in their oversized sleep shirts as noon approached. "They look like angels," he told me. Then he wrote up a hefty quote for a mitigation system, including a vent pipe, a fan, and the proper sealing of cracks.

What next?

According to friends who had experienced the military or worked for IBM ("I've Been Moved"), the next steps of relocation would be a snap.

"The packers will pack and label EVERYTHING!" one told me. "Even the trash."

True. The packers rocked. But then came the movers.

"Youse getting all fancy and moving on down to Jo-ja?" the driver said, loud and in my face, like the Big Guy he was.

The other one, smaller and wiry with dead black eyes, didn't say much. When he finally spoke, he was dismantling the once sturdy custom-made bunkbeds Rice and I had hobbled back together, with safety in mind, after a mishap.

"Whoever put these bunkbeds together should be shot," he snarled.

I said nothing but sent the kids down the street until the movers were gone.

Rice flew back the next day to help with last-minute details, then scooped up Jake, the cat, to fly back with him to Georgia. Oh, yeah, Rice and the cat flew South, leaving me to drive the kids *and* a goldfish named Strong One cross-country in Old Gray, our Ford Taurus wagon.

I remember only a few details. Like the click of my seatbelt seemed to signal one of the kids to drop something they couldn't reach but desperately needed. Oh, and I broke the drive into several days, partly so I wouldn't fall asleep at the wheel, but also to extend the excitement of our cross-country tour of various fast-food stops and gas station bathrooms.

Along the way, we detoured north to visit Rice's family in Lincoln, Illinois. The kids and I checked into the Holiday Inn and had dinner and a dip in the pool before turning in for the night. We visited Rice's family the next morning, toting Mel-O-Cream donuts and staying to visit for ninety minutes.

If this sounds odd or awkward, here's the thing. Families come in different flavors with different degrees of closeness. Rice's parents never visited us. Not once. For years we chafed about it, although I surmised it might be due to his mom's agoraphobia (undiagnosed, unless my skills in this area count). It was what it was. Except . . . Rice and I both carry tender memories of times with our own grandparents. So, if that 1991 detour to Lincoln conjures even a flash of warmth or fond thoughts for our kids, it was worth it.

By the time the kids and I arrived with Strong One in Georgia, I had convinced myself that the moving team would behave differently this time around. Maybe Dead Shark Eyes would find God somewhere between Colorado and Georgia?

They showed up to move us in on a Sunday, which also happened to be Rice and my twelfth anniversary. God love us. Rice slathered the kids' albino bodies with SPF and took them to the pool, where they melted into the hot, humid day while I supervised the move-in.

Big Guy sounded displeased that I didn't have pads to put on the floor beneath the legs of our baby grand piano. "Not good, Ms. Rice. People in Jo-ja like to keep their carpets nice."

Admitting he had a point, I made a note to pick up some pads at Home Depot.

And then something happened that reminded me why I liked these movers about the way I like pap smears and root canals. Meaning not at all.

As they were lugging a sofa off the van, a neighbor sprinted by on a jog.

"You wanna get some exercise?" Big Guy hollered after him. "Try moving this stuff. That's how *real* men get in a workout."

Oh, my God. No surprise, these *real* men didn't own up to leaving a gash on Timmy's entrance wall back in Boulder.

Trust me, the moving company got an earful. They took care of loose ends, sent me flowers, and vowed they would never contract with *my* guys again.

After the drama of the move, I hoped settling into our spacious new house in a cul-de-sac lush with magnolias, crepe myrtles, and Southern hospitality would go smoothly. Ha! Hope may float, but mine was lugging a heavy anchor.

Quickly, I learned that the balmy weather on our house-hunting trip in June had been an anomaly. Georgia's July was a hot, humid rain forest. One of the new neighbors outright snubbed me. (I'd bought her best friend's house.) And our big ol' backyard, perfect for fun and games, went unused. The neighborhood kids preferred to play in the cul-de-sac instead.

Lifestyle differences and culture shock snuck up on me daily. When I took the kids to the health clinic for school-required vaccines, the nurse counted the kids' teeth but didn't check their vision. Atlanta traffic sucked, and I discovered that while radon's not a problem in Georgia, termites are. Translation: more mitigation fees. Plus, we had fleas. Our house had freakin' fleas.

Even religious differences—among Christians, mind you—felt monumental. In Michigan, I'd attended a Lutheran church where I studied the Ten Commandments and loved Jesus but prayed to God. In Boulder, my eyes were opened to non-Christian faiths and the reasons we need to keep church and state separate. Now in Georgia, people often prayed to Jesus, not God, and my thoughts on separation of church and state were not well received.

Granted, I'm over-simplifying. The point is, I chafed, homing in on differences rather than trying to find common ground. I tried not to cry about all these cultural changes too much. But I felt like I didn't fit in with my Stepford wife neighbors. Did they *ever* leave home without a bra, mascara, and jewelry?

This damn move had been my idea.

But what in the world had I gotten us into?

· ♥ ·

Revisiting memories made and lessons learned thus far:

- Favorite wrong turn(s): The dozens of restroom stops we made during the cross-country move to Georgia by car. Every one of them was an accident avoided.

- Travel tip gleaned: The best time to travel cross-country with young children is . . . never.

- Insight into marriage: Laughing together can save a marriage. When it's hard to laugh, try to do it anyway. Even when it's through tons of tears.

Chapter 7: Family Discoveries ~ Along the Bible Belt's Back Roads and Beaches

Mid-1990s ~ Mountains and Shores, Georgia; Panhandle ~ Florida

A dapting to life in Georgia took time, but we learned quite a bit in the process. For one thing, Rice absolutely and truly does not like change. As for me, I *think* I like change, but in truth, I handle it pretty poorly.

And then there's the culture shock, which continued. I used to think jokes about Southerners hating Yankees were all in good fun. Guess what? They're not. At least, not in many a case.

Yet with time, we adjusted. A big fat saving grace came from how people treated our kids—with kindness, a sense of inclusion, and a joy in getting to know their individual personalities That neighbor who snubbed me at first? The ice melted through our kids. Quinn became best friends with her daughter, and in due time, she opened her heart to every last one of us.

When the neighborhood pool closed for the season, Rice and the kids settled in with their work and back-to-school activities. Off the bat, we discovered that Alex was academically behind—in second grade, for heaven's sake. Colorado's first-grade curriculum focused on reading and learning to print. Georgia first graders tackled those topics, too, but they also covered math and spelling and science and social studies. Maybe even trig.

As a Mom, I took ownership for this perceived shortcoming on my child's part. If only I'd known then what an incidental issue this would be in the course of a lifetime. But it would take me quite a few years to figure out that one.

By mid-September, the leaves began to change. Compared to Colorado, where the aspens turned a golden yellow, here in Georgia, a smorgasbord of color awaited around every bend. The earthy scent of fall encouraged weekend exploring. The Atlanta area offers an abundance of festivals and street fairs in autumn, like the Yellow Daisy Festival on Stone Mountain, again recommended by my sister Lynne. We attended, feasting our eyes on handcrafted pottery, woodwork, and jewelry while overstuffing our stomachs with corndogs, candied apples, and funnel cakes.

We also attended the Chomp and Stomp, an annual chili cook-off and festival along the streets of the artsy Atlanta neighborhood of Cabbagetown. A one-time old mill community, Cabbagetown now boasts beautifully restored shotgun homes and Victorian bungalows as well as funky little in-town eateries. Its Chomp and Stomp remains a family favorite.

One way or another, Atlanta's festivals kept us hopping. One Saturday we watched, wide-eyed, as fez-capped Shriners wove along Main Street in little clown cars during a parade in small-town Acworth. And we still carry proverbial scars from an outing to Piedmont Park, one where Quinn scooted down a hill on her back side, picking up a literal buttload of ants along the way. Rice thought quickly, stripped her nekkid, and whisked a cloth at her bootie until she was free from the ants. Maybe her dignity too. (If she remembers.)

Occasionally, we ventured beyond festivals. One of our most memorable outings that first year in Georgia took place in the spring. We easily found our general destination, the small town of Summerville, located in the northeast corner of Georgia, almost into Alabama. Finding Paradise Garden, home to folk artist Howard Finster and his work, proved more challenging.

I might not have even heard of the Reverand Finster if not again for my sister Lynne, who turned me on to his art shortly after our move. A former Baptist preacher turned self-taught artist, Finster produced 46,991 pieces of art, often of angels or pop culture icons or historical figures. Each piece was individually numbered. All contained handwritten faith-laced messages. Finster also created a 2.5-acre art environment filled with sculptures and repurposed items. He named this expanse—filled with tools and odd objects, antiques and curios—Paradise Garden.

I happened to own one of Finster's 46,000+ artworks. So why not visit his garden?

We headed to Summerville one sunny Saturday, figuring signs would lead us to Paradise Garden. Unfortunately, they didn't. And this was still before GPS navigation systems.

No worries, though. Finster was famous. Surely, someone could help us find the way.

We stopped at a McDonald's to ask for directions, but the clerk had not heard of Finster. Rice scowled, but undeterred, I asked again, this time at a gas station.

The young attendant pointed. "I think it's back toward the penitentiary."

"See," I said, feeling vindicated.

Rice followed the signs toward the penitentiary but soon determined we were driving in circles—or rather, big square blocks. The rural road of large lots and small ranch houses started to look repetitive. I tried not to pout as Rice pulled into a driveway to turn around.

He cut the turn short. Suddenly, we were stuck on a jutting drainpipe that connected the driveway and the ditch. No amount of Rice's rocking the car back and forth helped.

Daniel started to cry. (Sorry to narc you out, Dan, but you were little and understandably scared.) I walked the kids across the street to a vast green field, where a lady in curlers, a blue muumuu, and fluffy pink slippers was cutting grass with a tractor/mower. To be fair, Rice is not big on cussing; he leaves that to me. But at that moment, he was letting some mighty colorful language rip, so I walked the kids to the field mostly to get them away from their father.

The next part I recall like a slow-motion dream, not necessarily in chronological order. Our girls, digging around the fresh grassy field, found a four-leaf clover. And the muumuu-clad lady switched out her mower for a Caddy and pulled up behind Rice to offer a tow. I swear, she hooked up Old Gray to her Caddy and got it back onto the road at the exact time that clover appeared.

Daniel stopped crying. I shuffled the kids back into Old Gray as Rice thanked the lady profusely.

"That lady's an angel," I said to Rice as he finally got back into the car.

"You have no clue." He shot me a grin as he put the wagon back into drive. "She not only got us back on the road, but she gave me directions on how to get to Paradise Garden."

Her directions turned out to be spot-on.

We spent a crazy afternoon exploring Finster's property. It was just as creepy, amazing, and unforgettable as we had heard it would be. As extraordinary as our adventure to get there.

· ♥ ·

By the following summer, despite fears it might never happen, we had found a church home, and we joined our newfound friends for some misadventures in camping. With help from the more experienced among us, we found a site and pieced our tent together, because we wouldn't be Rices if we didn't discover it had missing parts. But, hey, we made do.

Over that summer, we camped two more times.

In my mind, I still smell the scent of fresh coffee perked over a campsite stove. A steaming mug of joe in the crisp early morning? Yes, please. Pair that with sizzling bacon and flapjacks. Could life get much better than that?

When dusk rolled around, the kids liked to gather around a crackling campfire. They'd share a few ghost stories, as long as they weren't too scary, and then they'd roast marshmallows for s'mores.

Talk about different personalities! Alex worked slow and steady, holding her marshmallow stick near the fire, just close enough to produce a perfectly toasted golden delight. Quinn tried to emulate her sister but usually ended up losing quite a few marshmallows to the fire. As for Daniel, his unspoken motto seemed to be, *Why roast them? They're perfectly good to eat straight from the bag.*

Then there was Rice, who had always enjoyed backpack camping in Colorado.

"Don't you like car camping in Georgia?" I asked him.

"I'm getting too old to sleep on a mat," he groused.

Easy peasy, I thought. All he needs is an air mattress for our next trip.

On that next trip, we also brought the family dog. We didn't expect it to rain. And rain. Imagine the smell of a crisp, cool rain in springtime, then consider this: That was not the scent that permeated from our wet, needy Irish setter on that hot, rain-soaked night in July.

We'd made camp at a site on Lake Allatoona, about half an hour from our house. As the rain continued, Rice suggested we drive home for the night.

"We can come back here tomorrow morning," he said.

I agreed, after the 80th time of jumping up inside the tent to knock the pooling water from its canopy. It didn't really cross my mind that he had no intention of coming back to the site *to camp*. Not until I heard him mutter the words, "Never again."

Long story short: That camping trip—The Adventure of Colo, the Stinky, Wet Setter Who Camped in a Tent on Lake Allatoona—proved to be the last one for the Riceman. For the sweet dog too. (But no worries. Colo lived on, just without any camping trips in his future.)

The kids and I made a few more lakeside camping trips on our own. I grew quite fond of Georgia's lakes—manmade, yes, but larger than Boulder's reservoir. True, none came close to the grandeur of Michigan's Great Lakes.

But that was okay.

The crown jewel of Georgia wasn't its proximity to the lakes, but rather to the ocean.

· ♥ ·

Jekyll Island, five and a half hours from home by car, became the first ocean getaway we chose. A one-time playground for folks with last names like Pulitzer, Vanderbilt, and Rockefeller, today it's owned by the State of Georgia. Only a third of it is developed.

We stayed at a nice enough hotel on the water, again in July, which, no surprise, was God-awful hot and muggy. We rented bikes, Rice and mine with seats in the rear for the Dudes (aka Quinn and Daniel). Alex was able to handle her own. We passed on attempting the fifteen-mile loop around the island, opting instead to follow paved trails, some meandering along the shore, others winding inland beneath massive oaks dripping with Spanish moss. We stopped at a convenience store for icy cold drinks. Mesmerized, we watched raccoons forage for food in the dumpster, oblivious to our presence.

Back at the hotel, the water beckoned. Because Alex loved the ocean, but the Dudes preferred the pool, Rice and I agreed to split duties. So, while I lugged sunscreen and floaties and swim toys poolside, Rice hit the beach. After a bit, we'd swap and repeat.

That plan lost its charm immediately, when Alex started to splash in the surf and Rice spied a dorsal fin skimming along the water behind her. He snatched her out of the waves right as the fin disappeared. It's hard to know for sure what he saw. Two rivers flow into the ocean near Jekyll, stirring up sediment that makes it hard to tell what's beneath the water's surface. Suffice it to say, we opted to stay near the pool for the rest of that trip.

Despite this, the next year we still heard the call of the ocean. We heeded that call once again and hit the road in Old Gray. Over the next year or two, usually during spring break, we tried out a few other beaches, like Hilton Head in South Carolina and Amelia Island back in Florida. We also visited my sister Susan in Lighthouse Point (Florida), where the kids learned to love fishing directly off her dock. Too bad Susan's place required a longer drive than the closer panhandle towns.

When a neighbor told me about Perdido Key, a barrier island on the Gulf that borders Florida to the east and Alabama to the west, we checked it out. Its waters gleamed, turquoise and clear as Destin's but with less of a crowd. We liked it immediately, returning to different condos in the same area the next few springs, until we finally settled on the Eden, an apropos name for our little slice of heaven on the beach.

It tickled the kids how their cheap ol' mom insisted we rent a condo *on the water* AND lease a pricy cabana for *the whole week.* They enjoyed lounging with me on the sand, reading and writing or sketching and dozing, safe from the sun's hottest rays as the tide rolled in and out.

Another treat for them was breakfast out with their dad. It became a game of which kid would he pick that day and where would they go? Maybe they'd drive for beignets in Orange Beach or they'd cross the street to a café where the sugar-sweet smell of pastries lured them in, but shelves crammed with board games kept them lingering.

Traditions evolved quickly, a favorite one our annual meal at Maguire's Irish Pub in Pensacola.

Recently, I smiled at a recollection I had from Maguire's, which I shared with Rice. "Remember how the kids loved to 'kiss the ass' on our visits?"

"Jan!" Rice laughed, choking a bit before he could continue. "I don't remember that. I do remember all the dollar bills, though."

One of the first things you see when you walk into McGuire's is all the dollar bills stapled to the rafters. Like many of guests before them, our kids joined the fun, writing their names on their own dollar bills and getting a stapler from the staff to put them up.

"But you don't remember the Irish band too?" I swear I did. "It got a little bawdy and sang a song with a chorus, 'kiss the ass . . . kiss the ass.' And there was a picture on the wall that had a donkey in it, and people would go up and kiss the glass of that picture."

He took a minute to Google Maguire's on his phone. "You mean the moose?" he asked.

"No." *Did I?* "Well, yes, I *do* remember the moose. But I also remember the donkey."

He looked at me for a minute and then shrugged. "Sorry, honey. I don't remember it."

Ugh. I stewed about it for a bit and then reached out to Alex.

"Do you remember the donkey?" I texted her. "I think you and your friend, Ariel, went up to kiss it. So it might have been during a soccer tournament when Dad didn't go with us?"

Alex texted back: "I think I remember that."

Before I got too excited at being right, I texted her back: "Are you just humoring me??"

"Does that sound like something I would do?" she replied.

I replied in a snap. "If you don't want me to think I'm senile, maybe?!"

She didn't text back, but so be it. I shared my story here, and I'm sticking to it,

We could almost predict how spring break would unfold. Alex would visit Urgent Care, probably for sun poisoning but maybe for strep. (We started to think our setter, Colo, might be a carrier. Alex *always* had strep.) Quinn would cry when it came time to pack for home. (She still loves the beach.) And Daniel would once again master the art of flying the kite, the same kite each year, the one we bought at a nearby shop that only stayed open for one season.

Old Gray delivered us safely to the Eden for several springs to come. We mourned when she passed from old age but replaced her with a Ford Aerostar, black as tar and boxy enough to be dubbed the Tank.

The Tank served us well through the years, too, lugging beach gear to the Eden while toting kids' sports gear, cellos, and drums back at home. The kids even learned to drive in the Tank. At 200,000-plus miles, it kept on ticking, our trusty mainstay for years to come.

In 2004, Hurricane Ivan struck Perdido Key, destroying much of what we had loved for so long. For quite a while, the destruction kept us away. When we did return—just Rice and I at first—it wasn't the same.

Eventually, we'd come to once again savor beignets and morning coffee out on the balcony. To laze beneath the overpriced cabana and to get that familiar kite to soar as high as Daniel had so many years earlier.

But it would take years—and our grandkids, Britton and Charli—to once again help us pilot that kite . . . and fall in love with Perdido Key all over again.

· ♥ ·

Revisiting memories made and lessons learned thus far:

- Favorite wrong turn: That sharp one that Rice took to get Old Gray stuck on a drainpipe somewhere near Summerville's penitentiary. It still makes me giggle.

- Travel tip gleaned: The tides may change, but with luck, you, too, may find a special place that beckons you back year after year. Fingers crossed, we have more years to come.

- Insight into marriage: Try to respect when your partner's tastes change (like, say, in camping). Even if yours haven't. Oh, and show some grace when memory slips occur. Because they will.

Chapter 8: Traveling as a Twosome Again ~ Chateau Elan and the Big Easy

Mid-1990s ~ Braselton ~ Georgia;
New Orleans ~ Louisiana

P lenty of couples do fine with one or even both partners taking on travel-intensive schedules for work. Rice and I didn't choose to be one of those couples. Up front, we understood Rice's new position in Georgia would involve several visits to company plants each year. That didn't strike us as too heavy-duty. But those visits came with surprises.

Surprise No. 1: I didn't realize that these power plants owned by Southern Company Services were *nuclear* power plants: Plant Vogtle near Augusta, Plant Hatch near Vidalia, and Plant Farley near Dothan, Alabama. The minute I heard the term *nuclear power*—around the time Rice was planning his first out-of-town trip—my mind went into a tailspin.

In Colorado, we had lived about thirty miles from the Rocky Flats plant, a nuclear power facility in Golden that fabricated plutonium triggers for nuclear weapons. I distinctly remember driving by the plant one time to see a protestor clad in a black body suit with a white skeleton encrusted over it, waving a sign that demanded: CLOSE ROCKY FLATS. It had unnerved me, reminding me of the Three Mile Island nuclear disaster in Pennsylvania in the late seventies.

Memories of nuclear accidents and Rocky Flats, which has since closed, left me unsettled the first half dozen times I kissed Rice goodbye to go visit his own plants.

Surprise No. 2: Rice's trips sometimes lasted up to ten days, stretching over the weekend. About the time I'd get the rhythm of doing the single-parent shuffle, he'd come home, and the dynamics would shift back to the way they'd been before he left.

Have I mentioned we're not a family that makes transitions easily?

During our early years in Georgia, I didn't travel with Rice often. Call me a diva, but I didn't feel compelled to tag along on his visits to the nuclear plants—not that spouses were ever invited. Also, I started some work-at-home ventures, which kept me busy. For a while I did medical transcription, then phased out of that to open an in-home music studio where I taught piano. Those gigs gave me the freedom to adjust my schedule, but it often meant working extra before and after a getaway if I wanted to be paid.

My work never made us rich. But it did help fund those trips to Perdido Key. And, despite the family's denials, I think they enjoyed coming home to Christmas tunes in October, plunked out in stilted rhythms by my piano students, wrong notes be damned. I *know* the Irish setter loved it. Often, he lounged on the music room sofa, belly up, content to pass gas and snore away while *Jingle Bells* filled the air.

Ah, the holidays.

Speaking of which . . . Rice and I had last attended a glitzy holiday party in Denver in 1983. I'd been pregnant with Alex then, so I'd passed on dancing with Rice, only to watch him knock a co-worker on her arse as he spun her around. Frankly, I thought (and partly hoped) the days of decadent company parties that included spouses had passed.

Then came the invitation to a December gala with one of Rice's work groups.

We puzzled a bit at the invitation, especially when another co-worker who did even more work for that group got left off the list. Should we pass on the invitation out of guilt?

Oh, hellz, no.

The event was scheduled at Chateau Elan, a winery and resort north of Atlanta in Braselton. Along with the RSVP card, the invitation included an embossed coupon for a discount on one night's stay. A substantial discount.

"Pinch me," I told Rice. If we could get an overnight sitter, we could do this.

I don't remember who babysat—my mom? my niece?—but I do remember that splendid getaway. We checked into the posh lobby, which smelled of rich wood and polished leather, and went directly to our room. It was spacious and elegantly neutral with high-end linens and deluxe bed pillows. The lavish bathroom was light and airy and housed fluffy towels, French milled soaps, and a bidet. Lah-de-dah.

We took our time, getting dressed up like grown-ups, Rice in a suit, me in a long red dress topped by a shawl. Giddy, we headed down to the ballroom. Rice saw a few familiar faces here and there but didn't recognize anyone at our table. Neither of us gave it much thought. While I waited in line at the carving station of the buffet, a friendly bystander spoke to me.

"You're Jim Rice's wife?" He was looking at my name tag.

"Yes, I am."

Then came a glint in his eyes. "Is he as much of a handful at home as he is at work?"

"Yes." I couldn't help but smile at this validation. "He is."

I didn't catch his name, and I lost sight of him by the time I got back to the table, where we engaged in more small talk, tasted some of Chateau Elan's unique vintages, and enjoyed our meal.

Toward the end of the evening, I nipped outside for a smoke and struck up a conversation with a woman who was enjoying the brisk outdoor chill for the same reason. I'd overheard her talking with someone else—someone who'd since gone back inside—and I gleaned she was the administrator who'd planned this event.

"This is a great party," I said. "I'm not sure how we got invited, but I'm glad we did."

"Thank you," she said, exhaling a puff of smoke. "But what do you mean?"

"Well . . . My husband does some work with this group, but not all that often." I shrugged, not sure what else to say. "I guess he's made a good impression?"

She glanced at my nametag. "You're Jim Rice's wife?"

I nodded.

She stared off for an instant, then turned her attention back to me. Her lips twitched a bit in the corners.

"There were two Jim Rices listed in the company roster I worked from. I wonder . . ."

I looked at her wide-eyed, not sure what to say.

"You know what?" She snuffed out her cigarette. "The other Jim Rice is a contractor. He'll probably never even know that he got overlooked." She shrugged, then stood tall and added, "If you don't tell, I won't either."

She winked and smiled, genuine and professional. Then she turned and went back inside.

· ♥ ·

If indulgent company parties were becoming less frequent, so were company-paid trips for out-of-town employee workshops and conferences. If Rice was lucky, he attended one event per year, usually with two others from his work group. Spouses weren't invited, so I missed out on Memphis, San Diego, and Orlando. San Francisco and Vegas too.

But something else was afoot. As the world approached the end of a millennium, fear of the unknown affected attitudes and behaviors. Some folks began to hoard money and bottled water. Others predicted that planes would fall from the sky one minute past midnight on January 1, 2000. Individuals who worked with computers—and spearheaded computer-run projects that *could potentially* run amok when phasing from 1999 to 2000—became a more valuable commodity.

Rice noted this. He added value to his own personal brand by learning the new-to-him Oracle software while remaining liaised with the older IDMS. This was a win-win for Southern and for Rice. He joined the IDMS Users Association and ran for its board.

"Guess what?" he asked me one day after work. "You're now married to the new IDMS Users Association President."

"I am?" Sometimes my gift for words, like *Congratulations!*, falls flat.

Unfazed, Rice continued. "Would you like to join the prez at an upcoming conference?"

I didn't ask where or when. "Hellz, yes!" I squealed as I hugged him.

For my first tagalong as the wife of an association board member, we stayed in the heart of downtown New Orleans at the Hyatt Convention Center. We could walk safely to the Riverwalk Outlets in the daytime. That's all well and good—for someone who doesn't get queasy in heavy humidity. Plus, with the July temperatures, I had difficulty moving gracefully in my drenched underpants.

We made the best of things, though, noshing our way through town, our appetites piqued by the smell of the holy trinity (sauteed onions, green peppers, and celery) on one corner, the strong caramel-laced aroma of chicory coffee from another We ate at the oldest family-owned restaurant, Antoine's. I'm not big on oysters or gumbo or Creole cooking in general, but I found Antoine's fish Amandine divine. We went on to savor other NOLA specialties, including muffelettas at Central Kitchen and po' boys at Mother's. And, yes, we did enjoy stopping for café au lait and beignets despite the heat.

Just in case it sounds like all we did was eat, please note, we also enjoyed Hurricanes down on Bourbon Street. Still, when I learned Rice's association had signed a contract to host its next five annual conferences at the same place and time, I told Rice no. I was one and done with New Orleans in July.

Even when the conference fell on our 20th anniversary, I refused to go. Rice went without me, the board sent me lovely flowers, and my friends fretted that divorce was eminent.

"Nah," I told them. "I'm pretty sure I saved our marriage by staying home."

Just sayin'.

In case you're wondering, I did return to New Orleans several years later, this time in April after our family's spring break trip to Perdido Key. Again, Rice had some kind of work thing. He flew out of Pensacola before break ended, and we agreed I'd drive the Tank—and the kids—from Perdido to New Orleans a few days later. Of course, because we are Rices, this trip had its shaky moments too.

Technology *had* made great strides. We'd survived moving into the new millenium, after all, and I even owned my own cell phone now. No GPS yet, though. Which is why, as we approached downtown New Orleans, I called the hotel to ask which exit I should take.

"Take the River Street exit," the clerk said. Or so I thought. But no such exit existed.

When it became obvious we'd passed downtown, I made a squealing U-turn. Wide-eyed and white-knuckled, the kids remained silent as I continued to drive while calling Rice.

"Where the hell am I?" I barked into the phone.

Of course, he had no idea. Lucky me, he remained calm and had me describe some landmarks, then managed to coach me on how to reach the hotel.

The kids still laugh about their mom's awesome driving in NOLA to this day. Not to my face, of course. But I swear I've even overheard whispered embellishments, like, "The Tank was veering on only its two left wheels!"

Geesh . . . kids.

In fairness, the kids handled the trip just fine, especially considering the Dudes were probably still a bit young for the town. The horse-and-carriage driver horrified pre-teen Quinn with his flirting. And Daniel horrified me with his curious fascination with a puzzle he found in a bodega, depicting a sex act I certainly didn't care to explain.

Still, we had a fun time. Sometimes you bloom when and where you're planted.

But in my case, that's never again going to be New Orleans in the summer. Sure, Bourbon Street's a gas. Just not in July.

· ♥ ·

Revisiting memories made and lessons learned thus far:

- Favorite wrong turn: Missing the River Street exit toward downtown New Orleans, but finding our way all the same.

- Travel tip gleaned: Clarify your destination, plus learn the time of year you'll be traveling before saying, "Hellz, yes!" to a trip.

(Oh, and get turn-by-turn directions to your destination too.)

- Insight into marriage: Choose a life partner who fills in your gaps. For me, that included finding a husband with an impeccable sense of direction.

Chapter 9: Cheers to Boston and Beaches and Broomsticks!

Late 1990s ~ Massachusetts

The year Rice got scheduled to tend to some late autumn business in Boston, I felt the earth move. Accompanying him to *Cheers* country in November versus the beignet kingdom in July? Yes! I lusted to go, even if it meant masterminding a plan with a zillion moving parts. Pesky things like getting kids to and from school, music lessons, and sports.

And dear Lord, would we have to obtain a second mortgage to cover travel expenses?

Just when I determined I really shouldn't go, I saw God. I swear I did. In the form of a roundtrip ticket from Atlanta to Boston on United Airlines for $99. On the downside, it was on a connecting ticket through O'Hare in Chicago. But back to the upside: $99. We booked it, Danno.

I'm not sure if alcohol helped or hindered, but I survived two flights and one connection, capped by a drive to a hotel in Westwood, Massachusetts, twenty-six miles from Boston's Logan International. Then at the precise moment we reached our hotel, Rice realized he had left a piece of luggage back at the car rental place.

"Wicked pissah!" I muttered, leaning into a Boston phrase, but with sarcasm.

"How 'bout this?" he said. "I'll drive back to get the bag while you settle in here."

Um . . .could I do that? Could I take off my mom hat, stuck snugly on top of my head, long enough to realize it wasn't my job to always "fix everything"?

Yup. I could and I did. This frazzled woman—me—who juggled a family and in-home piano studio with rare and random pockets of time to myself, settled into a room of my own, if just for the moment. With my notebook. And blissful silence. And space to think and make notes about anything and everything I wanted without interruption.

Ahh. The perks of traveling as "the spouse" were coming back to me.

Much like we'd handled Rice's work trip to San Francisco, I met up with him and colleagues and spouses to go to dinner at night. I didn't mind that Rice stayed busy with work throughout the day. I relished the downtime to read or write in the room, sometimes venturing to a nearby café or outdoor park.

A couple late afternoons, with Rice at the wheel, we made the twenty-five-mile drive into Beantown to check out recommended sites, like Boston Common and parts of the Freedom Trail. We shopped the Faneuil Hall Marketplace and ventured to Griffith's Wharf, where the states severed their ties to the mother country during the Boston Tea Party. (Yes, Mrs. Wendt, I *was* paying attention during the taxation without representation chapter.)

I truly enjoyed Boston, with all its amazing old churches and cemeteries and seventeenth-century architecture, like the Paul Revere House (built in 1680). And trust me, we made a stop to linger for beers and I snagged a sweatshirt at the Bull and Finch Pub, the old bar that provided the exterior backdrop for one of the best sitcoms ever, *Cheers*. The show went off the air in 1993. Thirty years later, I still take comfort in wearing that sweatshirt.

Of course, to every yin there's a yang, and here was Boston's: its rush hour paralleled Atlanta's, in that it lasted three to four hours on either end (as in 7:00 to 10:00 a.m. and 3:30 to 7:30 p.m.). Upping the ante, Boston drivers could use the emergency lane on the Interstate—legally!—when traffic got extra heavy, which seemed like always.

And then there were Boston's infamous roundabouts, or as the locals called them, rotaries. These special intersections (using circular junctions instead of stop signs to control flow) were new to us back then. I might have wet myself a little the first time Rice tackled one of them. He merged onto it with caution, not realizing Bostonians whipped around those things like they're a loop at the Indy 500. My knuckles stayed white for eons. But lesson learned.

No surprise, I chose not to drive in Boston, taking to heart one travel reviewer's eloquent words: "Trying to drive [here] will piss you off." Even in the city's beautiful downtown residential areas lined with stoic stately brownstones, cars still blocked traffic as people double parallel-parked, helter-skelter, anytime, anywhere they could find a spot.

· ❤ ·

"Why don't you take a spouse excursion?" Rice suggested a couple days into our trip.

"I could," I said. "But I'd rather explore at my own pace."

He raised his eyebrows, perhaps recalling that time I phoned him from the road to ask where the hell I was. But he said nothing. We both knew the score when it came to my sense of direction. Still, I wanted to venture out on my own.

And so, I did. Destination: Provincetown, Cape Cod.

I'm not sure what drew me toward the Cape and specifically P-Town. My love of water came into play, of course. It always does. Yet I'm pretty sure it went deeper than that. I'd read about it and expected to find a community that welcomed bohemian artists and writers as well as the LBGTQ+ community. Indeed, I found all that. But I learned some things too.

For instance, the Pilgrims first landed in Provincetown, seeking refuge from stormy seas, and stayed a month *before* moving on to Plymouth Rock. (I never read that in the history books.) Then came a period of P-town's Portuguese influence, a mix of fishermen, whalers, and Catholics, followed by the artists and writers. Today it boasts a robust year-round Jamaican population as well.

I visited at the perfect time of year—for me. Lots of the touristy spots had closed for the season. Yet plenty remained open, without the stifling lines. Bookstores and bike shops and artists' lofts beckoned. Places with names like the Lobster Pot buzzed with business. Sea breezes nipped at my ankles and kept the shopfront sidewalks dusted with sand. This was not the opulent Hamptons, which was more than fine by me.

My free-spirited, artsy, bohemian side—the part that often felt thwarted by living in a conservative northwest corner of the Atlanta suburbs—needed this outing. True, I *chose* to live where we did. And I've come to believe there are more good things than bad about it, and the South as a whole.

Still, sometimes things got to me. A couple years prior to my visit to P-town, my county's local officials penned and passed what supporters called a Family Values Resolution. Detractors—and yes, I was one—believed the resolution bred more hate than love, particularly towards the LGBTQ+ community. What constitutes family anyway? I wasn't alone with my concerns. Passing that resolution cost my county the privilege of hosting any events during Atlanta's 1996 Olympics.

I remind myself all this happened over a quarter century ago, in a time very different from today. But sometimes I wonder, is it *really* all that different now?

As for P-Town, I'd love to go back to experience it with Rice sometime. Its location, its spirit, its pulse. Plus, its abundance of small dogs and bikes and rainbow flags.

That Cape Cod road trip so many years ago nourished my soul in a way I didn't know I'd needed, enough so to prompt me to make another solo trip to explore. I mean, seeing how we visited Boston right on the tail of All Hallow's Eve, how could I *not* visit Salem too? After all, 'twas the season.

Driving into Salem, it struck me as more of a quaint village than a town. Its houses were built in first-period architecture common to homes in the late 1600s. The village itself sprawled across from the town Common, or, as we call it down South, the Square.

I started my self-guided tour at the Pickering Waterfront district and walked to the House of Seven Gables, the house that inspired Nathaniel Hawthorne's book by the same name. It's easy to understand how this lavish home with its secret stairs and hidden rooms managed to feed his muse. Even its gardens were splendid, although November meant a little less luster, like nary a wisteria arbor in bloom. I made do just fine with the seaside lawn and its picturesque view of Salem Harbor.

After leaving the House of Seven Gables, I wandered toward the jail and discovered an area with one-time residents' names engraved in bricks. I scanned the names until I saw PUTNAM, my birth name, etched on a brick. An aunt had told me our family roots wound back to Salem. I flushed at the thought as I moved on to peek at the Witch House, one of the last standing structures directly connected to Salem's most haunting history.

Salem may be the birthplace of Parker Brothers (the game company) and the National Guard, but it's likely best known for its heinous and infamous Salem Witch Trials. These began in 1692, after some of the young village girls claimed to be possessed by the devil. The courts believed the hysteria when the girls accused some locals of witchcraft, and twenty innocent people were put to death—fourteen women and five men were hanged; one man was pressed to death. (Drowning witches, or *swimming a witch*, prevailed in Europe, not Boston.)

I shivered on reading that history, then moved on to more cheerful things, like snapping a photo of the Elizabeth Montgomery *("Bewitched")* statue. I planned to frame it for Rice with a note: "Remember, you're not the only poor soul who married a witch."

Across from the Common, restaurants and shops bustled, opening their doors to everyday folks like me, but also to pagans and necromancers, some dressing the part, others more covert. A woman decked out in a black robe and pointy hat greeted me warmly when I stepped into her shop to sift through tarot decks, candles, and crystals, then onto mojo bags, witch balls, and jewelry. Biting back curiosity, I refrained from asking her whether she practiced the craft. After all, she didn't ask me about my religious practices.

Before leaving, I bought some postcards, a pentagram pendant, and a children's book called *WitchHunt: It Happened in Salem Village* by Stephen Krensky. Back in the car, I drove and the sights of Salem faded from my rearview mirror—houses with old pitch roofs and gables, towering over cobblestone streets. As traffic built up, I hated to leave that old-timey village behind.

Sighing, I scanned the highway and checked my side mirrors. With luck and a little more hustle, I could beat Boston's rush hour, which I did. But just by a whisker.

· ♥ ·

On the night before our return flight to Atlanta, thunderstorms hit the Boston area, wreaking havoc on flights already scheduled in and out of Logan International. The next day, the airport continued to play a game of scheduling catch-up, and Rice and I listened to flight delays and cancellations from our seats near the airport gate.

When we heard our gate agent offer $200 in flight vouchers to anyone willing to take a later flight, Rice looked at me.

"Should we?" he asked.

"I suppose we could," I agreed. We didn't have anything pressing from a time standpoint back at home.

"Never mind," Rice said, looking toward the gate. "It looks like someone else has already jumped on that offer."

A few minutes later, another announcement came over the PA system, offering vouchers again, but this time for $300 per ticket.

Rice rose to sprint to the gate to no avail. Someone else beat him to it.

He caught my eye and pantomimed that he was going to stay where he was, at least for a bit. It paid off. When another announcement came that delaying a flight would now be worth $400 in vouchers, he nabbed the deal.

I don't remember how much later our new flight took off or what we did while waiting. I do know that visions of future trips still danced in our heads as we boarded our plane to Atlanta.

We settled into our seats on the plane, still giddy from the excitement of our win. Still, that adrenaline rush did little to ease my flying jitters. To distract myself after takeoff, I ordered a glass of wine and looked through some reading material I'd tucked onto my carry-on. Finding the children's book, *Witch Hunt,* I followed along, entranced by the true-life stories of those involved in the madness and first arrests, the trial and secrets and doubts.

When I got to Chapter 6, *What Happened Afterward,* I sat up straighter. It told a harrowing tale of broken lives, of restitution without comfort, of how the girls of Salem Village were never questioned about their strange fits and visions. Only one of those girls ever came forward to speak about the events, fourteen years after the last conviction and death.

Goosebumps ran up my neck as I read her name.

Ann Putnam Jr. stood alone in front of a church in 1706. She confessed there had been no witches or specters. Fear and hysteria—and the need to find someone to blame—had caused twenty innocent people to die and many more lives to be irreparably ruined.

Years after that flight home from Boston, I learned more about Ann Putnam Jr. Her life remained hard. She never married but raised her younger siblings after her parents died. Among those siblings was a little brother born in 1695, two years after the witch trials ended.

His name was Seth. He was my sixth great-grandfather.

· ❤ ·

Revisiting memories made and lessons learned thus far:

- Favorite wrong turn: Learning I wasn't descended from Salem's persecuted but rather from their oppressors. Ugh.

- Travel tip gleaned: Yield the right-of-way to vehicles already in the rotary. And gauge their speed very carefully.

- Insight into marriage: The best life partners provide kind support but also patient space, allowing each other to learn to fix their own messes.

Chapter 10: Ooh La La ~ Any Chance We're Ready for France?

Late 1990s - Paris ~ France . . . with a Segue to Wurzburg ~ Germany

R ice likes to say he took me to France for $99. The truth is, I flew roundtrip *to Boston* for $99, and we proceeded to earn $800 in flight vouchers when we delayed our return to Atlanta due to a storm. Did my round-trip from Atlanta to Paris cost only $800? I don't know, but that's Rice's story, and he's stuck with it for over twenty-five years.

In Rice's mind, what better way to use those vouchers than on a trip to Paris? One puny problem: I didn't really want to go. I had visited Paris on a high school-sponsored trip back in the seventies, and at the risk of sounding like a privileged brat (which I was), I had hated it.

Granted, arriving there as a teenager suffering from a heavy menstrual period and nausea didn't help. Nor did the fancy dinner served that first night—fish with its scales and head and tail all intact. My next delight was watching a grown man pee in the street outside Notre Dame the next day. Then came the Mona Lisa, which no one had warned me was *très petite*. Talk about *une grosse déception*.

"It'll be different this time," Rice cajoled me. "You have a more sophisticated palate now. Plus, you'll appreciate the history and architecture more." He waggled his eyebrows. "C'mon. It's the city of love."

Eventually, I bought into his honey-soft sell, sweetened by promises that he'd ply me with plenty of wine throughout the flight. When we landed at Charles DeGaulle, I sobered up quickly, learning that French officials carry Uzis. At one point, they blew up an unattended bag. Not with an Uzi, but still.

City of Love, Rice had called it. I wasn't feeling it.

We lugged our baggage to the hotel, a place somewhere off Boulevard St. Michelle, between the Pantheon and the Sorbonne. My bags weighed us down, overladen with books and journals. ("Hardcover books!" Rice reminds me to this day.) As usual, I planned to read or write while Rice attended meetings, but on this trip, I'd do it while sipping café au lait near the Luxembourg Gardens.

Unfortunately, I felt myself starting to get sick. I tried to ignore my sinus cavities, which burned like a couple of brutal beasts. If I'd been home, I might have given in to the crud and stayed in bed. But I was in Paris. I didn't want to ruin Rice's time. Yes, I felt bad, but not nasty enough to keep me from getting out and about.

In Rice's free moments, we explored together, walking along the Seine and visiting the Louvre, Notre Dame, and the Musee d'Orsay. People all around us moved at a clip, whether rushing to work or walking their dogs. Crosswalk lights pinged. *Walk. Don't walk.* Horns honked and heels clacked.

It was . . . so metropolitan.

I tried to get into the Parisian spirit, snapping pictures outside the Métro and pubbing in Montmartre. We stopped for a bite at a bustling brasserie. Rice ordered a croque monsieur, which is supposed to ooze with ham and cheese and béchamel sauce. This one didn't. No big deal, though. Rice still loved everything about Paris. That's how he rolls, and I admire him so much for that.

"I would think you'd adore it here too." He winked. "Even if only for all the world renowned chocolateries!"

He had a point. With intent, I set my mind on moving past the crowds and the smell of carbon monoxide and cigarette smoke. And I *did* start to notice more chocolate shops, some family-owned, all high-quality, many just steps away from our hotel. On top of the chocolate shops, boulangeries and patisseries dotted the streets, filling the air with the scent of warm pastries and strong, rich coffee. If only I could have stuck with the chocolatiers and the truffles and gorgeous ganaches. I doubt that chocolate has ever exacerbated a sinus condition.

The night we dined out with Rice's colleagues and their spouses, someone chose a high-end spot in the Latin Quarter on the Seine near Notre Dame. A maître d' led us to a table with fresh flowers, crisp linens, and an abundance of plates and silverware. Soft music played. Feigning good cheer and sophistication, I scanned the menu, pondering terms like *"amuse-bouche"* and wondering if my palette had grown even *less* sophisticated than it had been in high school. Nothing sounded *or smelled* good. I felt a sudden odd kinship with our middle child, who often groused about restaurant food being *too fancy*.

I opted to order a salmon ravioli, presuming I'd get pasta pillows stuffed with cooked salmon and drizzled with light sauce.

I did not. When the *waiteur* delivered a plate of extremely undercooked salmon filets wrapped around pungent herbed cheese, I froze. Just the thought of my fork tines piercing uncooked fish texture made my stomach churn. I wouldn't have found that meal tasty even if I'd felt well. I love fish, but I don't like it raw. And being under the weather didn't help, not one bit.

"Would you like to trade entrees?" Rice asked gently, squeezing my thigh under the table.

My eyes grew wide. And watery. "Yes, please," I answered softly.

Confession: I've never forgotten that thoughtful and selfless act on Rice's part. That night, over a piece of raw salmon in a candlelit restaurant, I felt like I really *was* in the City of Love.

· ♥ ·

Rice didn't push me to go back to Europe. Not right away at least. He returned several times on his own, and his eyes sparkled when he shared his adventures. Viewing *The Last Supper* in Milan. Visiting Buckingham Palace, the Tower of London, and Westminster Abbey. Experiencing the natural beauty of Finland.

I enjoyed his international travels vicariously just fine. That MO, however—Rice traveling without Honey—didn't sit quite as well with him.

He started to nudge some more. "I'd like to take you to Europe again."

I stalled, singing him another verse about the difficulty of staying on track with my business and our teenagers' activities and school. In truth, I *wanted* to go enjoy Europe, but based on my track record, I had concerns. Rice was persistent, though, enough so that once again, I found myself on another white-knuckled flight over the pond. This time to Germany.

We stayed in Wurzburg, a charming Baroque city on the Main River, its streets studded with extravagant churches, chapels, and cathedrals. I was a bit more prepared for European proclivities this time around. Like the hotel's teensy elevator, where allowing a third person in with us required deep breathing on my part to avoid a claustrophobia attack.

Our first morning, Rice dug into the German-style breakfast buffet, returning to our table with a plateful of breads, cold meats, nuts, cheeses, fruit compote, and beans. As he sat, he mumbled something, or he just grunted. Immediately, one of the wait staff approached the table, eager to learn what Herr Rice might need.

"*Nichts, danke.*" Rice, who knew a little German, assured him he needed nothing.

The waiter laughed lightly and said, "*Oh, ich dachte, Sie wären Deutscher.*"

After he walked away, I looked at Rice, puzzled.

He shrugged. "I think he thought I was German."

Amazing. My man, who picks up dialects in a snap, now even grunted with a German accent.

One evening, we took a walking tour with a guide who pointed out the amazing architecture while sprinkling in fun little factoids. For instance, I learned the difference between a gargoyle and a grotesque. (The first is a decorative conduit for precipitation; the second is just for decoration.)

We passed by numerous *bier gartens.* As part of Bavaria, Wurzburg is chock full of them. Yet the city is also home to some of the region's oldest and finest Franconian wineries, producing fine dry whites. Our guide encouraged us to enjoy the wines, especially at Wurzburg's Juliusspital and Bürgerspital, which both use part of their profits to fund homes for the elderly, especially those needing rehabilitation. Nothing feels quite so nice as contributing to a good cause while eating and drinking one's way through a special city.

At the risk of sounding simple, the next day I asked Rice to help me map out a route with landmarks so I could venture out on my own. I didn't plan to go far. But *und oh mein Gott!* How I relished exploring on my own, people watching near the Marktplaz and gobbling down the best bratwurst EVER, right there on the street.

At one point during my outing, a gentleman approached me, looking very much like he had a question for me.

"No Deutsch," I said, not to be rude, but to save us both the time.

"Do you speak English?" he asked.

When I told him I did, he held up a piece of paper he'd written on. "Could you help me with directions, please?"

I grimaced. "Probably not." Might as well be honest up front.

At that, his shoulders fell. "Oh. I was hoping you could help me find the Dorint Hotel."

I grinned, realizing I *could* help him after all because we, too, were staying at the Dorint. I gave him the most detailed directions he's ever received in his life.

Later that evening, I don't know who enjoyed that anecdote more, Rice or me.

· ♥ ·

One day, Rice drove us through the winding German countryside. The driver's seat in the rental Peugot was broken, and we had to find a piece of wood to prop up the seat. No worries, though. These slower back roads led to several quaint towns around Wurzburg. Clean, quiet, and charming, they reminded me of the serene illustrations from the Hansel and Gretel story I loved as a child.

At lunchtime, we found a restaurant that specialized in Greek cuisine. The menu was written in German, and trying to communicate with the waiter, who spoke only Greek, proved challenging. Somehow, we patched together an order, not realizing that Rice had selected a cabbage-based dish . . . accompanied by an extra-large side of coleslaw. Holy gastrointestinal pain, Batman. It took him some time before he was able to enjoy coleslaw again. But we still get the giggles whenever we think of our special Greek lunch in Bavaria.

As for the best meal we had in Germany, hands down that would be our dinner at the Burgerspital, one of the largest wine estates in the region. The evening began with a tour of the wine cellars, brimming with Pinots and Reislings and Sylvaners, which we learned to recognize from the green teardrop-shaped Bocksbeutel bottles. So much history lay all around us, including the oldest bottle of white wine in the world, a 1540 Steinwein.

During the tour, we drank in the scent of butter and aromatics as we watched plates of food come together at the hands of the *herrs* preparing the courses. After the tour, we gathered in the wine cellar at a round oak table that seated all twenty of us. *Fraus* or *frauleins* served each of us seven courses, coupled with two different pairings of wine, which flowed nonstop.

Did I find some of the courses too fancy? I admit, the dove breast was just a bit rare for my liking. Still, what an experience. Our Sommelier described each food-wine pairing in German, then our host, Hans Peter, translated it to English as we indulged.

We lingered over the meal. And more wine. It was indeed a languid and lovely evening.

Back at the Dorint, several in our group stopped at the bar for a nightcap, but Rice and I retired to our room.

"I'm guessing tonight's meal was your favorite part of this trip?" I mused, taking off my jewelry as he fussed with the window sash.

"Until now." He stared out the window, turned to me with a grin, and beckoned me over.

I joined him and peered out the open window down to the courtyard below. Several guests lingered around a hot tub, some immersed in the water, others perched on the tub wall or just standing by to chat. They were relaxed. Happy. Enjoying one another's company, much like we'd done at our meal.

Except down in the courtyard, one thing was different. These folks were all nude.

Rice shook his head slowly, still smiling.

"Are you trying to tell me you want to go join them?" I asked, not sure how I'd respond.

"No." He laughed and pulled me close to him. "But, dear God, I love this city."

· ♥ ·

Revisiting memories made and lessons learned thus far:

- Favorite wrong turn: Going to Germany. I absolutely loved it.

- Travel tip gleaned: Don't leave your bag unattended at Charles DeGaulle, even to use the restroom. It may not be there upon your return.

- Insight into marriage: Don't give up on each other too easily. Change *is* possible. Just remember partners don't always work on the same timelines.

Chapter 11: One Last Family Hurrah ~ Before Time Slips Into the Future

Early 2000s ~ The Pacific Northwest ~ Oregon, Washington State, Canada

After Germany, my travels with Rice kept us closer to home. Finances played a part, as did the kids' ages and schedules, and I confess, my reticence factored in too.

And then there was my mother.

Once upon a time, we had relied on her to stay with the kids in our absence and use our car to transport them. We probably shouldn't have. She's passed on now—may she rest in the light—but I'm not talking smack when I say she was a terrible driver. It's true.

Looking back, the evidence snuck up on us. One time after she'd watched the kids, the gas cap went AWOL. Another time, the car felt exceptionally misaligned, and we heard the kids laughing about how their gram always bounced off the median when picking them up from school.

There were no giggles, though, when Rice and I returned from a trip and promptly received a call from our insurance agent.

"Hello, Janet," he said. "I'm calling for details about the hit-and-run accident you were involved in on [date]."

"What?" I gripped the phone so tightly I feared carpel tunnel syndrome would strike.

As the agent relayed information—the site of the incident, where and when it occurred—I realized the date he shared aligned with our travels. No mystery here. My mom was the culprit—er, I mean the driver.

When I phoned her about it, she replied nonplused. "Oh, that? It was just a little tonk."

"But you took off before calling the police?" I framed it as a question because I hoped our agent had been mistaken.

"I gave the other driver my information, just like we do in Michigan." Mom huffed. "I had to get home before the kids got off the bus."

I appreciate the value she placed on being there for her grandkids. But they weren't toddlers. I think they could have held their own if she'd tended what needed tending (like sticking around at the scene of a HIT and RUN accident).

In the end, we got the insurance company the information needed. Eventually. And if I'm not mistaken, we stopped asking my mom to sit for us right about then.

As the kids grew older, much of our travel included them. Shoot, most of our leisure trips piggybacked around *their* activities. If Quinn had a soccer tournament in Savannah, we enjoyed her games—and then hung out on River Street. When Daniel joined a creative problem-solving team through Odyssey of the Mind (OM), we'd tag along to explore or rediscover some of his destinations. Back in Boulder, we discovered a B&B run by Zen Buddhists that served vegan breakfasts. From College Park, Maryland, we made road trips to D.C. to see the Smithsonian, and Quinn and I snuck away for a special day trip to experience the Ocean City boardwalk.

As much as we could, we spent spring break week in Perdido Key. It never got old, body surfing and sunbathing, shopping for cheesy souvenirs, and pigging out on seafood. Alex was still able to join us there.

But she was getting older, working part time, and already missing some of our other trips. Soon, she'd leave for college, and we'd see her even less.

During spring break 2001, it hit me extra hard. Times, they were a-changin', baby. Around that time, three people I cared about died unexpectedly, all within a six-week period. One was a former boss, still in his fifties, who had been battling cancer, unbeknownst to me. He'd been a good mentor to me.

The other two were younger, still in their twenties, their days of promise snuffed out in motor vehicle wrecks. These events, especially the last two, shook me right to my core—and not just because I had teenagers learning to drive.

Suddenly, I realized the truth behind the cliché: Life can turn on a dime.

As a result, I stopped freaking out about money long enough to look at the bigger picture. After I did that, I booked us a big fat family trip.

We flew out of Birmingham, Alabama, into the Seattle-Tacoma Airport. Of course, it wouldn't be a trip with the Rices without a luggage gaffe or two. The first one happened before we even got onto the plane. It came compliments of Quinn, whose carry-on bag got pulled at the luggage screening area because of suspicious contents.

Rice was miffed. "Do you have any clue what's in your bag that would cause security to stop and check it?"

"No." Quinn looked genuinely puzzled as we waited impatiently for the security folks to do their thing.

Finally, security got to her bag.

"I'll be damned," Rice muttered as we all watched security unload several dumbbells Quinn had packed in her bag. He added to Quinn, "What were you thinking, packing those?"

"I was thinking we're going to be gone for a week," she said.

"Your point?" Rice's face took on a ruddy shine.

"Dad, how else am I supposed to stay fit?!"

She wasn't rude, just exasperated that he didn't seem to get it. And because he had never been a teenage girl, I'd venture to bet he probably didn't.

He exhaled loudly. "I was going to surprise you all with a stop at the Delta Sky Club. But now we don't have enough time."

The kids didn't seem too concerned. Then again, they weren't of drinking age, so they probably had no clue that the old man had been looking forward to a free cocktail. Or two.

Quick to regroup, Rice was his happy self again on the flight to SeaTac. Victoria . . . Oregon coast . . . Seattle—watch out! The Rices were on their way.

At the SeaTac luggage terminal, we worked an efficient assembly line to gather our bags from the carousel and then pick up our rental van. Rice was loading the bags into the back of the van when he suddenly stopped short.

"Shit!" he muttered.

"What's wrong?" I asked.

"I grabbed someone else's bag. Wait here. I'll be right back." He sprinted back to the terminal with the faulty bag, and we waited. I mean, what else could we do?

He finally returned to the van—with the right bag this time—and we hit the road toward Olympia.

"I made it just in time," he told me as he drove. "I went to the lost luggage kiosk where a couple was filling out forms to make a claim."

"And you got our bag too, right? So, life is good again."

No need to tell him the bag that had caused a thorn in his ass belonged to—you guessed it—the mighty Quinn.

· ♥ ·

We spent our first night in Olympia, partly because I loved it so, but also so Alex could check out Evergreen State College. The next day we whipped along Highway 101, which allowed us to experience the rugged nature of Olympic National Park. A long, winding rural road lush with trees and flowers led to Astoria, a quaint town on the Columbia River where the film *Kindergarten Cop* was set. We proceeded southward again, traveling along the coast, stopping at the Tillamook Visitor Center to sample some of the local cheeses.

In Cannon Beach, we picked up a picnic meal and headed for the beach, driving our rental van right onto the sand, just as I'd done back in college when visiting Florida's Daytona Beach. We tailgated on the beach, then drove to our destination for the night.

Schooner's Cove lay on another stretch of beach not too far from Haystack Rock. During low tide, folks would scamper across the sand out to the monolith to climb it. We stayed on shore, watching Alex sculpt a beautiful two-dimensional sunshine in the sand.

That evening, we lit a bonfire right on the beach, an experience oh-so-different from the Florida panhandle. Daniel helped tend the fire while Quinn wrapped herself in a blanket to cocoon against the wind. She made herself cozy in a cove-like area under a mammoth piece of driftwood.

I remember that stay fondly and still have a wine glass from our visit.

For our next stay in Portland, Rice and I had carefully selected the perfect lodging: McMenamins Kennedy School. Opened as an elementary school in 1915, it now housed fifty-plus guest rooms, converted from former classrooms, all complete with private baths. The place boasted a restaurant and brewery, multiple small bars, and a movie theater (popcorn, anyone?). Original artwork, mosaics, and old-time photographs covered the hallway walls. Old chalkboards remained intact in the onetime classrooms.

We waited for the kids to exclaim how much they loved their room.

"It's kind of creepy," Daniel offered.

Oh? Okay, looking back, their room had an Alice-in-Wonderland motif, which some folks (like me) do find a bit eerie. Not to mention, the movie *The Sixth Sense*, in which kids' ghosts roam deserted school hallways, had released just a year or two earlier. Geesh. No good deed . . . Thankfully, the kids got over the creepy factor quickly, and Rice and I relaxed in a separate room next door to them.

On this trip, we passed on stopping at Powell's City of Books. Its ten rooms, three floors, and 3,500 sections are a bibliophile's dream. Rice and I had visited during our last trip, but I was quickly learning you can't fit it all in every time.

Instead, we wandered Portland's Riverwalk, where the Rose Festival was underway. I mean, it had carnival rides, big ol' smoked turkey legs, and too many arts and crafts booths to count. Rice, being Rice, enjoyed watching his kids have fun. Meanwhile, I longed for a tiny pocket of peace as I sweltered in atypical 90-degree heat, wishing the raucous music and flashing lights from the various stages would just give it a rest.

Where was a quiet little bookstore—or even Powell's—when I needed it most?

On the way to Seattle the next day, Rice got a speeding ticket. He chafed.

"I forgot to slow down when the speed zone changed," he said.

"It happens," I said, intending to soothe him.

Of course, it didn't help when Alex added, "Doesn't it tick you off, Dad, when everyone's passing you, but you're the one who got the ticket?"

Rice drove the rest of the way like an eighty-year-old man. (Translation: very slowly.) Despite this, we arrived at the dock in time for our scheduled departure on the Victoria Clipper. The Clipper is known for its smooth sailing through Puget Sound, the Olympic Peninsula, and the Strait of Juan de Fuca. Usually. That day we encountered rough waters. For almost three hours, people kept getting physically ill all around us. It was delightful. But our family survived the voyage better than most. The worst part for us was when the door to the restroom flew open while Quinn was on the stool.

In Canada, we stayed on the fifteenth floor at the Chateau Victoria. Rain fell during our tour of the Butchart Gardens. Just a drizzle, but enough to make the firs, flowers, and grasses glisten like diamonds. We stopped in Victoria's Chinatown after the gardens, stopping first to visit the Victoria Bug Zoo. There, I kid you not, I thrilled the kids by holding a tarantula. Of course, we lost the disposable camera that documented my feat.

In Fan Tan Alley, we ate sesame chicken. ("The best ever!" Daniel claimed.) We toured the city by bus, catching glimpses of Craigdarroch Castle, Oak Bay, and the homes of the rich and famous. Ducks waddled all around the grounds of Beacon Hill Park, where black squirrels scurried in and out of the nature carvings. Back near the pier, Alex purchased a painting from one of the local artists. We capped the day by hanging out to see the Parliament Building all lit up at night. It was a glorious way to end an already lovely day.

Of course, no trip to Washington state would be worth a venti cup of Starbucks brew without a stop in Seattle. This may have been slightly after the grunge phase, but neither Alex nor Daniel had gotten that memo. While Daniel never met a flannel shirt he didn't like, Alex preferred to wear secondhand *anything*.

Her favorite thrift-store find was a blue and white pinstriped shirt—a bowling shirt, we surmised, because of the name *Gladys* embroidered above its chest pocket. She wore that the day we toured the Space Needle.

An older woman approached her and asked, "Where's the nearest restroom?"

Alex shrugged. "Sorry, I have no idea."

The woman just stared at her a moment, then mumbled something under her breath about young people and their poor work ethic these days. Then she stormed off, leaving Alex completely baffled.

"What did I do?" she turned to me to ask.

Pointing to the name on her shirt, I bit back a smile. "I'm not sure, *Gladys*. Maybe she thought you worked here." I no longer even tried to hold back my laughter. "Forgive me, but that may have been the highlight of this entire trip for me."

To this day, I still love the Pacific Northwest. Still, my reaction to Seattle left me feeling much like I'd felt in Paris. An apt description might be that I truly wanted to love these metropolitan cities the way most other folks do. Instead, my visits left me feeling a bit empty and . . . well, inadequate. I didn't like feeling like such a small-town girl.

I confessed this to Rice, who suggested we take a drive up the hill to Seattle's Queen Anne district, where the view of Seattle's landmarks made them look far, far away. Local shops and cafes lined the streets, along with ornate painted ladies. We sat outside a local shop to enjoy a non-venti cuppa while soaking up the vibes of intown neighborhood living.

"So, you're frustrated with yourself that you're not more of a big-city girl?" His blue eyes grew serious, but still gentle. "That doesn't make you provincial, you know? It just makes you, you."

· ♥ ·

Revisiting memories made and lessons learned thus far:

- Favorite wrong turn: Watching Alex tick off a tourist atop the Space Needle when she couldn't tell her where the nearest restroom was.

- Travel tip gleaned: Learn to adapt workout routines while on the road. Translation: leave the dumbbells at home.

- Insight into marriage . . . and life: When your spouse knows your travel preferences better than you do yourself—and accepts you anyway—consider that a wonderful gift.

PART III: Choose an Alternate Route

Chapter 12: Changes in Travel ~ When the Kids Start to Leave the Nest

2005: Manhattan ~ New York

In the early 2000s, I recertified as a Georgia teacher. Giddy, I signed a contract to teach sixth and seventh grade language arts. By the eight-week mark, I was living on five hours' sleep a night and I'd lost twenty pounds—despite my diet of Jolly Ranchers sprinkled with stress.

Around this time, something happened in class. In a fog, I *think* I told an extra gregarious student to *shut the hell up.* When one of my sweetest students gasped, it was confirmed. "That's right," I told the class, "I said *hell.*" I squeezed my fists and stomped my feet. *"Hell, hell, hell, hell, hell!"*

Then I wrote the kid up for class disruption and sent him to the principal's office.

I got reprimanded, as I should have. But that night, my mind and my heart raced. *Why had I lost my cool so badly?* To this day, I haven't been able to answer that question. All I knew was, this middle school teaching gig was *not* working. In tears, I typed up my letter of resignation. My tenure as a middle school teacher lasted eleven weeks.

Meanwhile, the world kept spinning. Hurricane Ivan struck in 2004, wiping out much of our beloved Perdido Key. That broke our hearts, but we stayed busy. The Dudes got involved with high school activities (Quinn, soccer; Daniel, orchestra). Alex transferred from Georgia State

University to a film school in New York City. And I enrolled at Kennesaw State University to earn a master's degree in writing.

Then came 2005, when Hurricane Katrina struck Mississippi's gulf coast. Over 1,800 people died or went missing, millions of folks lost their homes, and the cost of damages surged past the billions-of-dollars mark. New Orleans, the city I once loved to hate, became my obsession. In the blink of an eye, thousands of people's hopes and dreams got washed away.

The Katrina tragedy tore families apart. It reminded me that the time was now to get *my* family together. We could gather in New York, mother of all big cities. Why not celebrate family in the place that Alex now called home?

Granted, the thought of maneuvering the Big Apple *did* give me pause. Dealing with crowds, the din, how expensive it would be... It was a *city,* after all. Hadn't I *finally* made peace with the fact I wasn't an uptown girl?

Despite this insight, I sucked it up and embraced the circumstances. Alex shared a one-bedroom walk-up apartment with a roommate who'd be gone Thanksgiving week. Quinn and Daniel could stay with her. Rice and I had raked together money we'd saved from foregoing a beach trip the prior spring. Surely, we could find some budget place to stay nearby.

In a way, it felt immoral, arranging a pleasure trip on the tail of so much recent loss. Yet loss always tends to remind me that time is finite. What better way to honor those we've lost than to stop wasting precious time?

We approached our trip frugally, choosing to make it a thirteen-plus-hour road trip in the Tank, our boxy, black-as-ink Aerostar that *was* still ticking and kicking. We divided the drive into shifts—after all, we had four drivers—and stopped for an overnight stay in Hershey,

Pennsylvania. We ate at a Red Robin and chuckled that all the streetlights looked like Hershey kisses.

Upon our arrival in New York, Alex immediately made it clear I was acting too much like a tourist.

"I *am* a tourist!" I reminded her.

That didn't impress her. Come to think of it, I rarely did during her early adult years. She, on the other hand, awed me in so many ways, first by hoofing it up and down the three flights of stairs to her walk-up, repeatedly and without complaint. On top of that, she maneuvered her way with ease around the East Village, where she lived just three blocks from Union Square. Her ultimate superpower was coordinating logistics for us to catch the subway from different lines and still meet up together at planned times and destinations.

Speaking of the MTA, New York City's subway system . . .

Two solid memories come to mind. The first involves me and the big chunky orthopedic boot I'd been ordered to wear to correct a painful case of Achilles tendonitis. I was past any embarrassment over wearing it. Embarrassment dies quickly when you live in a house full of teenagers. Especially when an unnamed daughter—okay, the one still living at home—liked to mock me by strapping on my boot and parading around the house like a model on a runway, one arm crooked behind her head, the other at her hip.

In New York, my struggle with the boot came from trying to walk fast enough to catch the subway to get to our Thanksgiving meal on time. There was no rushing me and the boot. So, of course, we missed the first stop and had to wait for the next car. Lucky for us, the restaurant staff was gracious despite our tardiness—unlike *some* in our family.

My other subway challenge came because I can't walk and chew gum at the same time. Or, in this case, walk and carry hot coffee. I fretted about bringing it onto the subway car, but Alex gave me an irked look, as in, "Dear God, stop being such a tourist." A businessman sitting nearby glanced up, his own face bunched up in similar irritation, as if to say, "Old lady, don't you go spilling hot coffee all over me."

I set my jaw and refused to break eye contact with him. But, of course, I lost my footing.

As I was falling, I caught a glimpse of the man's expression. It looked like he couldn't decide whether I was going to scald him or . . . (I can only guess what he might have been thinking as my head did a freefall toward his crotch.) Yet the next thing I knew, an invisible force stopped me from landing flat smack in the man's lap. Turns out the force was Alex, who somehow grabbed me and stopped my fall without spilling her own coffee.

·♥·

Rice and I found a room at a Holiday Inn near Wall Street. We bid on it through Priceline, hoping for a room to ourselves, a little quiet, and maybe even a touch of romance.

The people in the room next door brought a little dog with them, one with the gift of yip, which continued nonstop anytime its humans left the room. So much for a little quiet. We still had our privacy, *and* we could get romantic if we so chose. So, we took to heart the title of an old Meatloaf song, "Two Out of Three Ain't Bad," and we made do.

Some highlights from our Big Apple trip? I learned that stoops are NYC's version of porches, just smaller. (I'd always wondered what a stoop was.) Also, rats scurrying along the subway rail are *not* uncommon. (Actually, I might not have even seen the first rat if Alex hadn't pointed it out to me. My girls could be special like that. Both of them.)

While in the city, Rice wanted to try out Katz Deli, home of the famous orgasm scene (with the *I'll-have-what-she's-having* line) from

When Harry Met Sally. A sign at the door warned of cash-only transactions, so Rice scampered down the street in search of an ATM.

He may have underestimated how much cash to get. Or maybe my sense of cheap kicked in. All I know is we ended up getting one sandwich to go and splitting it up back at Alex's. *Ah, New York*, where the sandwiches were huge (sixteen ounces of meat) and pricey ($27.45). A fifty-dollar bill wouldn't have covered two sandwiches plus tip, even in 2005.

The highlight of our New York trip was attending the Macy's Thanksgiving Day Parade. We snagged a spot in Central Park and marveled over the larger-than-life balloons and all the great bands and entertainers—even the Radio City Rockettes. The winds gusted so strong that a huge M&M balloon swung out of control, striking two sisters who sustained minor injuries. We learned about this on the news, hours after it happened. Thankfully, everyone else survived the parade winds just fine.

After the parade, we stopped to warm up in Rockefeller Center. At FAO Schwartz, Daniel and I tried out the life-size piano keyboard, the one that Tom Hanks and Robert Loggia danced on to plunk out a version of "Heart and Soul" in the movie *Big*. We didn't do too badly ourselves.

Our most poignant New York moment came when we stopped to remember lives lost at Ground Zero, the site of the Twin Towers terrorist attacks of 2001. Standing where it all happened brought goosebumps, taking this pause to ponder the unstoppable spirit and resilience of New York and its people.

Where else can you witness so much culture and such an eclectic mix of people living side by side? I mean, Indians, Irish, Italians, Chinese, Koreans, Dominicans, Puerto Ricans, Caribbeans, Hasidic Jews, Latin Americas, Russians and more, all living side by side. It blew my mind.

Trust me, I'm still no uptown girl. But I'll always treasure our family trip to NYC.

· ♥ ·

Revisiting memories made and lessons learned thus far:

- Favorite wrong turn: Going back to teach in 2003. My failure with that taught me so much and eventually pushed me back toward a career in writing. (Side note: Don't ever diss teachers in my presence. They absolutely, positively walk on water!)

- Travel tip gleaned: No matter what you do when traveling with teens, you'll always embarrass them.

- Insight into marriage . . . and life: When you see your teenaged kids, arms linked together, skipping down the streets Manhattan with glee, you forget all the pain-in-the-ass moments they've put you through. Only for a moment. But it's enough.

Chapter 13: Changes in Travel
Part 2 ~ Tripping Around Even
More of Life's Milestones

Late 2000s ~ Washington, D.C.;
Annapolis ~ Maryland

The family trip to New York City served as a bridge to a new stage in life for Rice and me. I finished my master's and went back to work full time as the grants manager for a nonprofit legal agency in downtown Atlanta. Quinn left for Georgia Southern University (September 2006), and Daniel started Georgia Tech the following fall (2007).

I looked forward to yet another new chapter. For Daniel, of course. But for Rice and me, too. Before entering this empty nest stage of life, we had scheduled vacations around kids' breaks. Now we had absolute freedom, if not unlimited funds, to travel when we wanted.

Except . . . a new stumbling block tripped up our travel plans: my grant deadlines. This became a BIG point of aggravation for Rice when he realized he had more unused annual leave days than he could roll over.

"How did we let this happen?" he grumbled.

Of course, we both knew how. My irrational fear of losing my job over a missed deadline made it tough to plan any significant chunks of time away from work.

"Can't you just re-negotiate a deadline in a pinch?" Rice asked, wide-eyed.

Oh, sweet man. If only.

Something had to give. And it did. Rice and I began to schedule more short getaways. We started to once again piggyback on out-of-town conferences. This time, our travels got built around *my* work, not his.

Rice tagged along with me to conferences in Chicago and San Francisco, where I once again left my heart. A work trip to Vegas provided us the opportunity to see the amazing Elton John live at Caesar's Palace. Tickets cost as much as an extra mortgage payment, but the experience was worth every penny.

Yet if I had to name the best getaway linked to *my* work, hands down, I'd choose D.C. I'd choose it even though it's a big ol' city. Not to mention, the conference took place in July, when D.C. felt as hot and sticky as New Orleans.

Off the bat, Rice's devotion to public transportation vexed me. Instead of hailing an air-conditioned cab, we dragged our bags from D.C.'s Dupont Circle Metro Station past several embassies to get to our hotel.

Once settled in, we formed a plan. While I attended sessions each day, Rice could re-visit the memorials honoring Lincoln and Jefferson, World War II and Vietnam. He could stop by the Capital Building or the National Archives to view the Declaration of Independence and the U.S. Constitution. I love his fondness for history, but a little bit goes a long way for me.

"Did you get to see everything you wanted?" I asked him on the group walk to dinner the next night, after he'd told me about his day's stops.

"As much as I could," he whispered back. "Just know if I'm walking funny, it's because I'm so chafed between my legs, I could die."

I raised my eyebrows, then shot him a wink. "Your secret's safe with me." *Poor guy*.

Several Atlanta attorneys who sat on my organization's board had come to the conference, too, and we dined with four of them that first night. Their banter energized the blood in Rice's old college debate veins. At one point, I sensed he'd completely forgotten about the chafing between his legs.

"Feeling better, are we?" I whispered.

He grinned. "I'm feeling great."

Pretty amazing how a little fine wine, a delicious meal, and great company can suddenly make life good again.

· ♥ ·

On the last morning of the conference, Rice took the Metro to pick up a rental car from the airport. I waited in the air-conditioned lobby, grateful my times of toting luggage were done.

Except they weren't.

When we arrived in Annapolis, parking was scarce. We found a public parking deck and then dragged our suitcases several blocks to a tree-lined residential section. We came upon a group of tourists clustered in front of a plain-looking old white building. Their guide pointed to it, and I could only make out parts of what he said. ". . . on the National Register." Then he added, ". . . originally the home of Thomas Jefferson's physician."

Not in the mood for a history lesson, I turned my attention back to Rice and grumbled, "How far is this place?"

"We're here," he said, nodding to the Victorian home the guide was discussing.

Stepping into the Annapolis Inn was enough to make me quit grousing. Listed on the National Register, it's just steps away from the historic capital and harbor. It consists of three guest rooms, each on its own floor. Rice and I stayed in the third-floor Rutland Suite, complete with a wood-burning fireplace, a king-sized bed with Italian linens, a sitting room with a built-in window seat, and a private sundeck overlooking a garden. Its bathroom housed a clawfoot massage therapy tub, a stall shower, bidet, heated floor, and towel warmer.

It would have been easy to hole up in that room and never come out for the rest of our stay. But we would have missed so much if we'd done that, starting with a peek at how the Naval cadets survived in the barracks. Those living quarters were very small. And neat. Incredibly neat.

From the barracks, we walked to the quaint downtown, with its 300-year-old buildings chock full of shops, galleries, and restaurants. We passed a street fair in progress, grabbed a late lunch at the Middleton Tavern, then returned to our room to get ready for the night's outing, which Rice had planned as an anniversary surprise.

"You'll see," was all Rice would tell me when I asked about the evening's agenda. "But it's recommended that you wear sneakers."

Um, no. I may not have been a fashionista, but this was before the advent of vogueish sneakers. I tossed on some blingy flipflops and followed my man. If I were a squealer, I would have made a scene when he led me down the dock toward the Woodwind II.

"You're taking me on a sunset sail?" I sucked in my breath, looking around the deck of the very schooner sailed by Christopher Walken's character in *The Wedding Crashers* movie.

Of course, in predictable Rice style, a glitch occurred. Before we could set sail, a storm blew in—no thunder or lightning, just rain—but all of us, passengers *and* crew, had to cram into a place in the hull to seek refuge. Six of us squeezed together near sleeping quarters we learned could be rented for overnight sails.

"What do you think?" Rice whispered, arching his eyebrows as if to ask: *How would you like an overnight sail on the Woodwind II?*

"Oh, hell no!" I blurted. God love me, my claustrophobia was kicking in.

When a few of our fellow passengers shot me some sympathetic smiles, I presumed they probably heard me.

Rice didn't miss a beat. "What a great way to get closer to people. In the hull of a schooner, stuck at a dock on the Chesapeake Bay."

The threat of the storm passed quickly. Back on the deck, Rice bought champagne, and we sipped it, overlooking the water and the sunset. An Asian Indian family was also onboard, celebrating their patriarch's seventy-fifth birthday. Feeling festive, we poured a glass of bubbly for him too.

On the horizon, spits of lightning warned that another storm brewed. We made it back to the dock safely. I never doubted we would, but I'm not sure Rice shared my confidence. He put on a brave front, but I've come to realize that he likes boats about as much as I like planes. God love my sweet landlubber husband. Knowing him the way I do makes it even sweeter, the fact that he took me out sailing to celebrate our marriage.

P.S. My blingy flipflops handled the sail just fine.

· ♥ ·

Back at home after that trip, Rice and I started to talk about moving. We pondered whether to downsize into an in-town neighborhood that would put us both closer to work. Then in late 2008, the housing market crashed, and our relocation discussions lost their luster.

The following summer, 2009, I changed employers, going to work for the public health department closer to home. I still worked in fundraising and wrote grants, but conferences weren't in the budget, at least not at first. This probably wasn't bad timing, given that more changes brewed on the home front.

Our newest challenge in two words: my mother. Again. But this time in a different way.

Concerned, Mom's neighbors in South Carolina had reached out to my sister Tina. Mom's cognitive skills were slowing. Plus, had she mentioned to us that she'd had a mini stroke?

Why, no. No, she had not.

With three of her five daughters living near Atlanta, we convinced her to relocate here. She bought a condo in Sandy Springs, a lovely place with a balcony overlooking the pool and the courtyard. It offered independent living but also tiered assistance, like a group meal option and a PCC (patient-centered care) floor. What a godsend that was.

Mom did well for a bit, but she was prone to falls. Especially after enjoying a bit too much vodka. One of her tumbles required shoulder surgery, which then called for several weeks at a rehab facility. She was *not* a happy or compliant patient. Nor was the rehab facility one of the more stellar ones. At one point, we discovered the cords to Mom's call button had been tied to her bed frame, making it impossible for her to reach if she needed it.

We called in an ombudsman to ensure this practice got discontinued.

Later that day, Tina said, "I have friends who've already gone through similar things with their aging parents." Her brown eyes lost a touch of their light. "It can go on for years."

She was right.

Mom's cancer diagnosis came in the aftermath of a visit to the ER after she had fallen. My sister Lynne learned the full diagnosis—ovarian cancer—while Rice and I were in Perdido Key. She hated to ruin our trip by calling with the news, but I was already in a funk, having discovered many of the family's favorite old haunts had been razed by Hurricane Ivan. Not to mention, a beach trip without the kids just felt wrong.

More change awaited us. Our son Daniel married his high school sweetheart Lauren and moved to Tulsa. Our daughter Quinn got pregnant. *(Surprise!)* Work demands continued, as did Mom's appointments and chemotherapy sessions.

Looking back, we call those years our time of Amazing Grace. It's apt. My mom's name was Grace, and she was amazing, in too many good, bad, and crazy ways to describe.

We did the best we could, balancing the demands of everyday life and work and an aging parent. In the end, time *does* run out. Maybe the key is to keep on living the best way we can for as long as we can?

It's a simple plan—but an incredibly hard one to execute.

· ♥ ·

Revisiting memories made and lessons learned thus far:

- Favorite wrong turn: No favorites here. Just a fork in the road that involved choosing whether (and how) to care for an aging parent. I wish I could pass along a map or a how-to manual, but it's not a one-size-fits-all endeavor. Trust me.

- Travel tip gleaned: Travel while you can—as much as you can. You never know what lies around life's next corner.

- Insight into marriage . . . and life: Focus on loving life and the ones you care about the best way you can at life's different stages. Yes, it's hard. Do it anyway.

Chapter 14: Is This a Respite or a 9-1-1 Incident?

Early 2010s ~ Dadeville, Alabama

I feel like I'd be remiss if I didn't disclose one special good-time getaway Rice and I shared during my mom's last year of life. Amid demands and burnout, a co-worker offered Rice the use of her lake house for a weekend getaway. (Thank you, Linda Wilson!) We're not always comfortable taking up offers like this. But her place on Lake Martin in Alabama was a mere three-hour drive. (Not to mention this was around the time of our thirty-third anniversary.)

We were on that offer, baby. Dare I say, like white on Rice?

It was the perfect getaway. Rice and me. A lake house—beautiful, rustic, chic. The water—clear, aqua, expansive. The air smelled of rain and freshly cut grass as we strolled down the sloping lot toward the water. A couple icy adult beverages and some down time on the dock were just the ticket.

Spotty cell service? No problem. We were on the water. Lake Martin, Alabama. Ahhh.

Eying the jet skis tied at the dock, I called dibs on the red one. (As if Rice would ride the other one!) I named that red jet ski Stella, then bragged to Rice about how the next day, Stella and I would go out and spin double nickels! (That's code for fifty-five, my pending age at the time, and the speed limit I was ready to push.)

"Why wait?" Rice asked, his grin wide.

The next thing I knew, I was bouncing across the lake, wind and water whipping my hair. It was pure heaven. I found the marina, which Linda had described as "just beyond the point," and I gassed up Stella for the next day.

Back out on the water, I hugged the shore closer this time. Feeling the waves beneath me, I passed colorful clusters of Adirondack chairs . . . cozy cottages . . . American flags flapping in the breeze. Then I passed them again. And again. Meanwhile, black clouds loomed. Lightning flirted, about to flicker.

Was I scared? Only a damned foolish ninny wouldn't have been.

As for Rice, he grew uneasy as darkness began to set in, wondering where in the hell I was. He even drove to the nearby marina where he learned that I'd stopped there for gas . . . over a half hour earlier.

When he returned to the lake house, I was still gone. Under his breath he cursed me for leaving without my phone, despite . . . well, spotty cell service. Not to be stymied, he called the police to ask if they had suggestions for tracking me down on the lake. To his dismay, officers came to the house, walked him down to the deck, and peppered him with questions, shining their flashlights into the dark depths around them.

Meanwhile, out on the lake, which happened to run sixty-eight square miles across three different counties . . . I was lost. So lost I couldn't even sniff my way back to the marina.

I tried not to panic. But how could I ask anyone for directions when I couldn't recall the address or the name of the subdivision where we were staying? It didn't enter my mind right then that perhaps I should ask them to call the police to help me out. For heaven's sake, I couldn't even recall Linda's last name at the moment.

Also, lakes don't have shiny green glow-in-the-dark signs like roads do. So, if I asked for directions and someone told me to veer right at Turkey

Creek (or Moonshine Cove or wherever), that would not help me one bit.

Still, what else could I do but ask for help?

Spotting a father and son casting lines from their dock, I inched Stella up, close enough to share my woes. Perhaps they noticed I looked like a deer in headlights when they tried to explain the way back to the marina. Against claps of thunder, these angels powered up their boat and led me back there themselves.

At the marina, I asked another boater if I could borrow a phone to reach out to Rice.

Alas . . . I think I've mentioned spotty cell service?

Needing to gather my wits, I went inside the marina shop to buy a healthy snack. (Okay, I bought a wine cooler and cigs. Don't judge.)

"Are you Jan?" the clerk asked.

I raised my eyebrows. "Yes?"

"An elderly gentleman stopped in an hour or so ago," he continued. "He was worried about his wife Jan out on the water."

Oh, my dear, sweet man . . .

But oof. *Elderly gentleman?* At the risk of going to hell, I admit, that made me snicker.

I shouldn't have laughed, though, because apparently, I think much the way an elderly gentleman does. Trying to figure out ways to connect back to Rice, I also thought of the police, and I asked if someone could give me a ride to the station.

The next thing I knew, I was in a jeep, jostling around back roads of the lake with two young guys I'd never met before in my life.

Had I not seen enough episodes of *Law & Order* to know better?

Blame it on the wine cooler. Or the optimism of youth—theirs. When these guys *promised* me they were good Samaritans and *insisted* they knew the lake and could find Linda's place, any danger radar I had failed me.

"Can you remember *any* landmarks?" the driver asked.

Breeze rustled my hair, helping me think. "A little chapel, maybe?"

He took a few turns, and the other guy asked, "*Any* road names?"

Suddenly, I envisioned a street sign that Rice and I had passed earlier. "Peckerwood!" I blurted.

"Wow, Jan," one of the guys commented. "What a thing to remember."

Yes, I was mortified *that's* the particular thing I remembered. Yet seconds later, we turned onto Peckerwood Road. And, in short time, we *did* find the lake house.

As the jeep pulled into the driveway, the guy in the passenger seat turned to me. "Do y'all drive a white vehicle?"

"No," I replied, wondering why he'd asked.

When the driver muttered, "Oh, shit," I saw what I hadn't seen before: a white deputy's vehicle parked in the driveway.

The jeep engine idled as the front door of the lake house flew open. Rice rushed out onto the driveway, two law officers on his tail. He looked ashen from worry—indeed *elderly*. For a moment, I thought he might chew me out. Instead, he lumbered over and hugged me. Tight.

The officers and my young rescuers left PDQ. It had to do with their open containers, but I felt bad the young guys hightailed it before we could even offer a reward.

Minutes later, Rice shook his head while mixing us extra strong gin and tonics.

"All I could see were the headlines," he said. "*Georgia Man Arrested After Wife Disappears on Alabama Lake.*"

He handed me a glass, and I studied him—flushed, relieved, slap-happy. Both of us were.

"Perhaps that was your plan all along?" I ribbed him. "To lose the wife."

Before he could respond, I had a slightly more serious thought. "After all these years, how could you not remember that I get lost everywhere, even in my own driveway?"

"Oh, honey, I know!"

Okay . . . he didn't have to agree to that with quite so much gusto.

"I'm sorry," he added. "I just saw how happy you were to be near the water and . . . I wasn't thinking."

"It's okay." I reached over and brushed the top of his hand. "I got swept up in the moment too."

To Rice's credit, he didn't attempt any further comeback.

As for me, I must admit I found it a little bit sweet that, thirty-three years into the marriage, we both could get swept up in a moment—the same moment and at the same time.

Together.

· ♥ ·

Revisiting memories made and lessons learned thus far:

- Favorite wrong turn: Finding that marina to begin with. It had to have been by sheer dumb luck because I still don't know what a point is in lakespeak.

- Travel tip gleaned: Quality getaways don't have to be far, far away or last forever.

- Insight into marriage: It's sweet to overlook a partner's shortcomings. But when said partner has no sense of direction, think twice before encouraging a jet ski joy ride at dusk on a massive lake with 750 miles of wooded shoreline.

Chapter 15: A Pause for Amazing Grace ~ Celebrating A Life Well Lived

Fall 2012: Brutus ~ Saginaw ~ Michigan

In spring 2012, I took to carrying my cell phone in my bra. Classy, I know. But with our daughter Quinn being pregnant and a mom prone to losing her step, I needed twenty-four/seven access to incoming calls. If I wasn't wearing something with pockets, what was I to do?

"Don't mind me," I told the paramedics, tending to yet another of Mom's falls. "But if my boob starts to vibrate or ring, it most likely means that my daughter's in labor."

I never received such a call, but all for good reason. On her doctor's advice, Quinn had scheduled a C-section. So, we marked our calendars, knowing we'd spend April 4th welcoming our first grandchild, a baby boy named Britton.

We anointed ourselves JJ and Big Daddy, and from the start, I was smitten. My mom was, too, when Quinn and I drove Britton to meet her when he was two weeks old.

I helped her hold him and asked, "Do you remember his name?" Her memory had become a roller coaster run amok.

She thought for a beat. "I want to say, Melvin."

"Gram!" Quinn sputtered. "I gave birth to an infant, not an eighty-year-old man."

We shared a good laugh over that. Even Mom, although I suspect she might have joined in the chuckling just to be part of the camaraderie.

A week later, I got a call from one of Mom's caregivers in the wee hours.

"I need to know who to call about your mom's final arrangements," she said.

As much as I thought I was ready for that call, I wasn't. (Are we ever?)

We held a small, private, local service at Mom's advanced care facility. And then we got to planning a more apt celebration of her life.

· ♥ ·

The first part of celebrating Amazing Grace took place on Burt Lake. It's in the "up north" part of Michigan, near the tip of the middle finger of the mitt. (Awkwardly stated, but true.) Mom had always loved the water, despite never learning to swim. She also adored when her daughters' families gathered to enjoy one another without her prompting. Funny how moms of adult kids all love this. Dads, not so much. I suspect it has to do with a word that starts with a *d* and rhymes with llama.

What can I say? Family gatherings often *do* mean drama, and Burt Lake proved no exception. But mostly, I remember the good parts.

My sister Lisa, who still lived in Michigan, found a lake house big enough for most of the family to stay. That meant renting a smaller place, also, one with two bedrooms and a loft. Probably not intended for three couples, but we got by. God love Daniel and Lauren for taking the loft, but they were the youngest couple. Rice and I, along with Lisa and her partner Mitch, completed the small-cabin gang, which I'll refer to from here on as the Lucky Six.

We spent most days at the big house out near the water, where we swam and made sandcastles on the shore. With two babies under a year—one of them my niece's, the other one Britton—we fit in plenty of snuggle time, often outside on the hammock. Lisa and Mitch brought his pontoon, Old Bull, which they docked at the small cabin each night, then used to transport the Lucky Six to the big place each day.

All of us found a way to contribute, whether brewing the morning's coffee (thank you, Tina), helping cook or clean up after a meal (thank you, Susan), or making the daily pie run (curse you, Rice). Oh, yeah. The Riceman discovered a place in town called House of Pies. When I rib him about all the pies he bought, he sniffs. "I don't recall anyone complaining."

A new surprise awaited when we discovered the Tunnel of Trees, a stretch of M-119 surrounded by hundreds of very large hardwoods. Tree tops from both sides of the road touch in the middle to form a ceiling of leaves. Driving under this lush canopy in summer feels like taking a ride in a fairytale forest. I can only imagine it in autumn.

For most of our visit, we hung by the lake, soaking up rays on Old Bull, some of us enjoying craft beer or red wine while we floated. We kayaked the rolling blue waves and played countless games of cornhole. During one round, "someone" performed an accidental pirouette, which led to a broken toe. I won't mention names. (But c'mon, do I *really* need to?)

We ended most days with a bonfire. And sometimes before the Lucky Six headed back to our digs, we enjoyed some ass-whomping card games. Mom would have loved that part. It always made her happy to see her girls and their gangs getting along.

After several splendid days celebrating her life and memory on Burt Lake, we headed back to Saginaw, where Mom had spent much of her adult life. Lisa had reserved space at the Anderson Enrichment Center, a frequent wedding venue, and we had arranged for food and drink to be brought in for 150 guests.

On the drive to Saginaw, a minor crisis unfolded in in the car when Quinn grew concerned that four-month-old Britton had not had a bowel movement for almost two days.

"Does he seem bothered?" I asked. "Or uncomfortable?"

He didn't. But his mom was another story. Especially when Britton's dad searched on Google to learn causes for chronic constipation in infants.

"Hey," Patrick said. "Have you been mixing Britton's formula with that spring water we've been drinking? It says here it can cause a mineral overdose . . ."

The rest of his comment got lost to a loud noise coming from Britton's direction. And just like that, all the calm, sweet moments we'd enjoyed on Burt Lake came out in one explosive instant.

On the downside, the stench in the car was immediately unbearable. On the upside, we'd just arrived at our destination.

Dare I say everything—and I mean EVERYTHING—came out just fine for Britton that day. I can't say the same for whoever had cleanup duty. If I recall correctly, my friend, Joni, showed up to save the day. God love her, with umpteen grands of her own, she barely flinched.

Inside the Anderson Center, friends and family gathered. Daniel and Lauren, who'd flown in from Tulsa, played a moving duet of "Amazing Grace" on their cello and violin respectively. My niece Erin delivered a lovely homily. And then guests stood and shared their own special memories.

We'd decorated the tables with flowers, and Lisa also brought in Mom's scrapbooks, one for each table. It seemed apt. The woman had compiled albums of pictures and memorabilia collected throughout the years, including what seemed like every greeting card she'd ever received.

But here's the part I love most. People chose where to sit as we ate and drank and listened to people's shared memories. After much of the speaking was over, I heard a stir at one of the tables where several of my old high school friends sat.

"Oh, my God," my friend Joni exclaimed, pointing at one of the pictures in the album open on their table. "That's us!"

Turns out the album on that table covered the part of Mom's life when she'd been up to her elbows in raising teenagers. Tina, Lisa, and me . . . and some of our friends on occasion too.

A similar reaction occurred when some cousins discovered their table album contained pictures of them. They grew misty over favorite memories of Aunt Grace, who'd apparently doted on them more than I realized after I went off to college.

I still get a chill at how all this unfolded. None of the albums were labeled. Guests chose their seats at random. Yet time and again came the murmurs.

"That's me!"

"Awww, that's Grace and me back in the day."

I've always wondered if Mom was looking back through the light to witness her loved ones sharing their cherished memories that day. I hope so. Even today, I smile at the thought that her spirit *might* have had a hand at guiding people to where she wanted them to sit. She always loved setting a fancy table and orchestrating an over-the-top celebration.

· ♥ ·

Revisiting memories made and lessons learned thus far:

- Favorite wrong turn: Indulging in spring water directly from nature. It's a special treat for many, but definitely not for infants on formula.

- Travel tip gleaned: Six adults, three bedrooms, and one bathroom in a small cabin stinks. Literally.

- Insight into marriage . . . and life: The journey comes smack full of zigzags and setbacks and, yes, even heartbreak. So don't forget to laugh.

Chapter 16: Celebrating Just the Two of Us Again ~ The Trip of a Lifetime

2014: Italy

"I want to take you to Italy." Rice surprised me with this out of the blue.

"Italy?" I hadn't heard him mentioned Europe lately, and certainly not specifically Italy.

"Two weeks of small towns in Tuscany." He winked. "Maybe Lake Como too."

Mmmm. It sounded romantic. Fine food. Wonderful wine and art. George Clooney. *But two weeks off work*? Visions of missed grant deadlines made me almost queasy.

"Think about it," he said. But we both knew I wasn't quite ready for two weeks away.

On July 21st that year (2014) we celebrated thirty-five years of marriage. Because we're the Rices, a massive Federal grant application was due by midnight on that same date. Just in case I ran into last-minute snags, I suggested to Rice that we plan on a low-key evening at home.

"Don't worry, though," I told him. "It's pretty much good to go."

True. I had the grant narrative down to perfection. Ditto the logic model and budgets, the tables and a zillion attachments. I had everything in hand except for a Memorandum of Understanding (MOU) from one of our partners, outlining their part in the project if funded. Without that signed MOU, our application would be disqualified.

What was the holdup?

My boss. I could hear her on the phone from her office next door, negotiating that MOU like a pit bull. Finally, around 7:30, she won her case and brought me a signed agreement.

"Good teamwork," she said.

Easy for her to say. She got to go home then. I had to stay and finish uploading the application.

All the way home, I seethed. Once there, I planted a long kiss on my frustrated husband's lips. Then I pulled away gently and stared intently into his baby blue eyes.

"Book us on a freakin' trip to Italy," I said. "And do it tonight! Before I change my mind."

· ♥ ·

We flew to Milan mid-October. Since our lodgings on Lake Como weren't available until the following night, we planned a detour. We caught a train to Lugano, which cradles the Alps on the southeastern tip of Switzerland near the Italian border. We checked into Hotel International au Lac, into a room with a beautiful waterfront view from our balcony.

Holding hands, we window shopped nearby places too rich for our blood, like Hermes and Prada and Louis Vuitton. We dined outside at a place called Tango. I don't remember the food, but folks sipped on drinks that looked like Orange Crush in a wine glass.

"We'll have what they're having," Rice told our waitress, who brought us our first Aperol Spritzes, which, to this day, remain a favorite summer libation.

The next day, we celebrated Rice turning sixty. We spent the morning lingering over breakfast, shopping, then touring an ancient church with frescoed walls still full of color despite their age. We strolled by children at play in the park and caught a glimpse of two men swimming in the lake.

"Oh, look . . ." I pointed to one of the men, the one wearing a Speedo.

Rice didn't miss a beat. "Maybe I should get one of those?"

I had no words.

Shortly after our stroll, we caught a bus from Lugano to Varenna. It wound through mountain roads, rugged and narrow and, frankly, scary. Beeps from other buses warned our driver to make way. Squeals and sputters from passing vehicles made me grateful that Rice wasn't driving.

We crossed the Swiss Italian border into Managgio. From there, we caught a ferry to Varenna, a small town on Lake Como's eastern shore. Our host, Paulo, met us at the dock, and we had to be quick to keep up as he walked us through narrow cobblestone streets lined with medieval architecture. My blingy flipflops were killing my feet by the time we reached the building that housed Casa Mara, Paulo's rental home, which he'd named after his wife.

On the bottom floor of the 300-year-old building, a watercolor artist ran a studio-gallery. I made a mental note to buy some of her postcards. (And also, to wear walking shoes from here on out.) We climbed many steps to reach our charming third-floor apartment. Grapevines covered its balcony, which had a side view of the water.

Most of our days in Varenna started with breakfast at Bar il Molo, in part for its better-than-average Wi-Fi but also for its ambience. Despite the cool mornings, we sat outside, overlooking the rippling water, snuggled in blankets the café provided. We savored the coffee, piping hot and so strong that I needed to add milk. Over bacon and eggs for Rice and pastry for me, we'd linger, planning our day while young school children skipped on by, filled with chatter and laughter.

One day we rode a ferry around to the different isles on Lake Como. None compared to Varenna in beauty, not even Bellagio, where we walked and walked—and walked—and ate lunch at a place called Baba Yaga.

Back on the ferry, I tried not to stare at a nearby couple, mauling each other, deeply in lust. I glanced Rice's way and rolled my eyes. He looked back at me with a grin that said, *What the hell! We're in Italia!* I nestled closer against him and stayed that way for the rest of the ride.

We hiked a lot in Varenna, one time to see Fiumelatte, Italy's "shortest" river, where the water misted our skin as it pattered against rocks in its path. Another time we trekked a distance to Castello Vezio, with its sculptures and "ghosts" made of gauze and chalk draped in fabric. Nearer the heart of town, we paused to watch a couple exchanging vows at the end of a dock. Dressed in a simple gown, the bride carried a small bouquet. It struck me as the most perfect wedding. Discretely, I snapped their picture before heading back to Casa to dress for dinner.

While I thought we'd probably eat some meals in, Rice wanted none of that. And I get it. The food was sublime, whether small meals of wine and antipasto or big evening feasts that sometimes included a primo course (usually pasta) *and* a secondo (often fish). In Varenna, reserving a table meant it was ours for the night. The *whole* night. So, we'd linger over each course, with lots of laughter and conversation in between. Wine too.

After dinner our last night in Varenna, Rice suggested we get gelato. I'm not sure how I found the room, but I did. Good thing, too, because Italian cows produce the most magical milk.

That night, a warm, dry wind swept through, reminding me of the chinook winds we experienced in Colorado. Come morning, we packed up our things and made our way to an inn near the trains for coffee and pastry. We ate in silence, each of us wondering how the rest of our journey could ever live up to Lake Como.

· ♥ ·

The train ride to Tuscany passed vast farmlands. We wondered if folks really lived in the spare-looking farmhouses, or if they drove in from elsewhere to tend the land. Unlike our train from Milano, which traveled at 300 km—186 mph—the ride into Chiusi was slower. Rice called it a milk run. It stopped at least a dozen times to pick up kids returning home from school. We enjoyed the slower pace, watching the teenagers—too cool for school in any country—move on and off the train and about their day in their own way.

We picked up a rental car, a Fiat, in Chiusi. Rice had bought a GPS chip for English translation, thankfully. (That was state-of-the-art technology back in the day.) Still, the Italian street names rolled out so long and luxurious that often we'd pass our round-about exit before the speaker finished telling us which one to take.

We arrived in Montepulciano and checked in for our stay at Vicolo Dell-Oste. Most mornings I woke up first, and I'd sit near an open window of the main room, sipping cool water, enjoying the crisp air that billowed the curtains. On the alley-sized street below, locals opened their shops and swept their entryways. A trash truck did duty one morning, chugging by, small and efficient. Even in paradise, someone needs to deal with the garbage.

Our host, Luisa, insisted we visit Sienna to see the Duomo, with its breathtaking mosaic floors that told stories from the Bible. Parking was sparse there. From the time we left our car until reaching the site of the Duomo, we had clocked over 10,000 steps. One way.

"This is grueling, having to walk so far," I muttered.

"What can I say?" Rice replied. "There was nowhere closer to park."

"Well, we should have checked about getting a taxi."

"Oh, c'mon," he cajoled. "It's not that bad."

Less than an hour later, over lunch, I heard the young women seated nearby mention how grateful they were that they'd taken a cab. These women appeared to be half our age. I looked pointedly at Rice on hearing their conversation. His return smile, slightly chagrined, told me he got my message.

The next day I told Luisa we loved Sienna, but if it was the biggest city we visited, I'd be happy. I waited for her to tsk-tsk about how we'd miss too much culture if we skimped on visiting the cities. Instead, she pulled out a map and made us a route of smaller destinations.

A funeral mass was in session when we arrived in Pienza. We could tell from the formal dress of the people gathered, the solemn hum of their conversation, and the languishing toll of the church bells nearby. Dogs howled in response to the church bells as we wove our way into town, careful not to disrupt the proceedings.

Wildflowers lined Pienza's alleys, and cut flowers popped from vases adorning apartment windowsills. As we ascended the streets into town, sounds from a very good jazz duo filled the air above the Cathedral. Nearby, a middle-aged couple swayed in a dance.

We followed Luisa's special-marked tour like participants in a road rally, albeit a very relaxed one. Her map led to sweet little stops filled with local culture but without the fanfare of tourist destinations. No mandates, like "you must stop here" or "you must eat there."

Italy helped me realize that the thing I love most about travel is watching everyday folks lead their ordinary lives in extraordinary places. And by extraordinary, I mean different. Different from what I am used to.

For instance, in San Quirico d'Orcia, a youth soccer team jumped from a couple of vans at the same time we arrived. We just watched them and took in their energy, which filled the air, as did their boisterous shouts, their physical pre-game jumps and sprints. We trekked behind them into town, then veered our own way to browse the quaint storefronts and watch through the window as a barber cut a little boy's hair in his one-man shop.

Our next stop was Montalcino, where believe it or not, a wine festival was in progress. Colorful flags flapped overhead, and laughter and lively music filled the air. For a bit, we tried samples of wine while watching some high-energy college-aged men engage in a tug-of-war ceremony. Then we found a place near Bagnes Vignoni, the old Roman baths, where we dined and experienced some of the best wines of the trip: a 2004 Brunello and a French vintage, too expensive to try to remember its name.

Every stop provided more delights. In Volterra, we walked parts of the old Roman theatre, which held close to 3,500 spectators inside its medieval walls in ancient times. Excavated in the 1950s, its stone rows jutted through patches of green that looked as soft as moss.

In another part of Volterra, an elderly couple sold us chestnuts they roasted right there on the street. They looked like they might have come from another time, their faces ruddy from years of toil, their heads wrapped in sweat rags, their drab gray clothes hanging too loosely. The man tended the smoky hot ovens, while the woman wrapped their goods in brown paper and tended their till. I'd like to say the chestnuts tasted delicious, but I don't recall, which means they probably didn't. What I do remember is the couple, working side by side to sustain a life they'd built together.

We enjoyed Montepulciano itself plenty too. Its narrow streets brimmed with shops and wine bars that served delicious house blends, crisp crackers, and Pecorino Toscano, a cheese made from sheep's milk. Pedestrians ruled the streets, which had secret corners around every bend.

And then there was Montepulciano's food, which was ah-maz-ing.

Our most unique dining experience took place at Osteria Acquacheta, famous for twice-nightly group seatings and fabulous T-bone steaks. We sat at a communal table, where small talk buzzed. A young couple stuttered through English to share that they were new parents, and this was their first evening out. We gushed about this trip, our once-in-a-lifetime, we liked to call it. Another couple our age replied that they'd visited here four times . . . and sometimes they just craved a taco or some kind of food that wasn't Italian.

We ordered wine, and the chef paraded by, toting a platter heaped with raw slabs of beef. One of two young Asian women seated near Rice giggled at the size of the steaks.

"Mostly I eat vegetarian," she confided, shyly.

The man who loved tacos laughed out loud. "You won't tonight," he told her.

The steaks arrived at the table, a bit on the rare side for my liking. The young vegetarian dug into her meal with pleasure, praising the chef and looking like she'd never had a better meal in her life. I tucked that memory in a corner of my mind, hoping I'd eventually develop as much grace as she displayed at that dinner.

Our most intimate meal—and my favorite—took place at Godimento di Vino. A sommelier/restaurateur in a burgundy apron greeted us, led us into the small dining area, and seated us at a table for two covered with a green-and-white checkered tablecloth. We were surrounded by glass walls, which allowed us to gape into a cellar paved with stone and filled with casks of wine and countless bottles as well.

The sommelier/restauranteur doted on us and the one other couple seated nearby. The man at the other table talked loudly. I'm not sure why, but I found his manner a bit pompous. When he observed that we spoke English, he took that as an invitation to start a conversation.

Oh, great, I thought. There goes our sweet little intimate dinner.

But as Rice—my *better* half in this instance—engaged with the man, I softened. He spoke Italian and English but, naturally, was most fluent in his native German. Rice enjoyed putting his German lessons to use, sharing a bit of conversation with him. The woman, we learned, spoke only Greek, so the man did his best to translate our conversation to her in Greek. Listening to all this humbled me and made me a little ashamed that, since high school, I haven't ever considered buckling down to learn another language.

What did we order? I have no recollection. I'd go back in a heartbeat, though. That night in Godimento di Vino, I finally *got* why Rice loves to travel abroad. It's not for the landmarks. Or the terrain. It's not even for the fabulous food. Those are *all* lovely, yes, but we can *enjoy* a decent share of those things right here in the States. And for a lot less money.

Rice's love of travel boils down to getting to know people. There's no better way to open our hearts and our minds to this crazy old world unless we first open up to her people.

For the last leg of our Italian adventure, we dropped by Pisa to take kitschy pictures and buy Rice a scarf. From there, we continued to Cinque Terre, the "poor man's" Amalfi Coast. Rice inched the Fiat along narrow roads. I prayed that he'd keep his hands steady, as one false jerk of the wheel could send us down jagged cliffs and into the aquamarine Mediterranean Sea. The view of the towns and the piers and the colorful homes along the water was stunning. For the record, though, if we do a future trip, we'll take the train from La Spezia.

Would we do another trip to Italy? Yes, please! Personally, I would extend our time in Cinque Terre to see more of her five villages and enjoy another seafood feast at Miky in Monterosso.

Then again, so many other places are calling. Not to mention, we don't think we left much red wine behind when we returned from that first trip of a lifetime.

·♥·

Revisiting memories made and lessons learned thus far:

- Favorite wrong turn: Italy had none. Unless you count driving to Cinque Terre.

- Travel tip gleaned: Our world is a big crazy mix of people, cultures, and geography. We make it smaller—and better—when we bridge our differences rather than dwelling on them.

- Insight into marriage . . . and life: Might not work for everyone, but thirty-five years into our marriage, Italy made us feel young and in love again.

Chapter 17: Celebrating Three Generations ~ Cruising Into a Calamity of Errors

2016: The Bahamas ~ Haiti ~ Jamaica

"Let's visit someplace overseas every year," Rice suggested in the afterglow of Italy.

"How about every five years?" I countered.

With only five years left until retirement, I figured now was the time to renovate a few rooms and do some landscape updates. Travel money not spent could go toward sprucing our place up, getting it ready to sell if we decided to downsize. Or to enjoy if we opted to stay.

Rice agreed with my counteroffer, and we christened 2016 the year of the kitchen. We selected a contractor, made a downpayment, and purchased materials. Then Rice got a call from Patrick, our daughter Quinn's boyfriend. Could he come over to talk with us?

"Son of a gun!" I sputtered to Rice. "Patrick's going to propose."

"I would think you'd be happy," he replied.

He had a point. Patrick's a good guy. He and Quinn had been together forever. Five years earlier, when they'd discovered her pregnancy, I suggested that surely, they'd want to get married *then*. In an intimate ceremony in his parents' backyard.

"Marriage is a big commitment," they each told me on separate occasions.

"I know," I murmured, keeping the next part in my head, all to myself: *SO IS HAVING A FREAKING CHILD!!!*

But back to Patrick and our supposition he was on his way over to announce his intentions.

"Are you going to give him a hard time?" I asked with a grin.

"I don't think so," Rice replied. Then it was his turn to grin. "Listen, you'd better make yourself scarce. Patrick didn't ask to come talk to *us,* only to *me.*"

To his credit, Patrick honored tradition, getting the patriarchal blessing he knew his bride-to-be and her father would adore. And suddenly, mid-kitchen renovations, we had a wedding to plan.

Both Quinn and Patrick wanted to have an intimate destination wedding, a Virgin Island cruise followed by a larger reception later back home.

"Would you like us to watch Britton while you're gone?" I offered what I would have wanted had I been in their shoes.

Not Quinn. "I've never been away from him overnight," she said softly.

Maybe the time has come! I wanted to say. Then I remembered the mantra a friend chants when her own married children make choices she wouldn't: "It's their story now."

"Whatever you'd like," I said, trying to mean it.

Rice smiled broadly and echoed, "Absolutely, whatever you'd like . . . as long as it includes me getting to give my daughter away!"

He was not so ready to give up a co-starring role in their story.

Oh, holy shit. Then and there, the wedding planning began. And this ol' gal, the cranky lady who doesn't like pomp and circumstance or spending outrageous amounts on travel, led the charge.

· ♥ ·

Because Quinn's a teacher, she and Patrick proposed a seven-day cruise to coincide with her school district's fall break. They chose a cruise ship, *Allure of the Seas* with Royal Caribbean. I convinced Rice we should pay for the whole family to be there—the wedding couple and their son, of course, but also our other two adult children and their partners. In my mind, the whole family needed to be there to witness Q and P exchange vows on Magens Bay in St. Thomas that September.

I surprised myself, enjoying this wedding planning more than I anticipated, first by helping to shop for bridal gowns, then by helping with the STDs. That's Save-the-Date cards, for those not in the know. Of course, being the Rices, after mailing them out, we discovered an issue. Not a big one, mind you.

"Um, Mom?" Quinn said over the phone in that little voice that foreshadowed potential trouble. "You know all those STDs we filled out and mailed from the beach?"

"Yes, what about them?"

"Wellllll." She drew the word out for what felt like forever. "We forgot to include the wedding date."

I wish I could say she was kidding, but she was not.

It was all good, though. Life went on.

I made a deposit to work with the cruise line's wedding coordinator. When I learned that we wouldn't discuss actual plans until two weeks before sailing, I decided that wouldn't do. I demanded a refund and contracted with an off-ship private wedding planner instead.

Oh, yeah, I was Jan with a plan, even purchasing cruise insurance for every single last one of us in the family. We had, after all, scheduled our sail at the peak of hurricane season.

Everything played out well leading up to departure. Granted, Rice continued to grouse that everyone was flying but us. (We'd been warned that the airlines couldn't promise to safeguard the wedding dress, so you-know-who and his wife agreed to drive it to Ft. Lauderdale.) And somehow, after years of teaching young children, Quinn contracted her first case of head lice—the week before we were to leave. No worries, though. She found a company called Lousy Endings, and they eradicated the problem.

We departed Ft. Lauderdale in the sunshine, which I took as a good omen. It wasn't until our first port stop that I realized what a huge ship we were on. I felt almost queasy, getting off the ship in Nassau, part of a cattle call with 5,000+ other passengers. The clouds and patches of rain didn't help lift my spirits. Some of the kids opted to climb the Queen's Staircase, but Rice and I checked out St. Watling's Distillery. A couple rums in, I grew more relaxed. I *would* enjoy this trip, by golly. How could I not?

Hours later, back at sea, Rice and I relaxed even more over martinis in our stateroom. The path of Hurricane Matthew—which we'd been watching like hawks, trust me—didn't appear to be headed toward St. Thomas. We began to lean into the excitement of the upcoming ceremony.

When the captain made one of his daily announcements, I only half-listened. I was too busy daydreaming about the next day, when a gentleman clad in Caribbean garb would beat out intoxicating rhythms on his steel drum. But then I noticed a scowl forming on Rice's face. He put down his drink and shook his head. My breath caught as I tuned in to parts of the captain's ramblings, still coming over the muffled sound system.

"... Hurricane Matthew ... need to reroute ..."

I looked toward Rice for a sign that I'd heard things incorrectly, but he just continued to shake his head. We didn't speak for some time. I mean, what was there to say? The cruise route wasn't our call to make. It was the captain's.

And the captain had already spoken: *Goodbye, St. Thomas. Hello, Haiti.*

I poured over that cruise insurance we'd purchased. Dammit. It didn't cover rerouting. Still, the younger Rices and guests swore they could fix things.

"We can pool our funds," one suggested, "for a ceremony in Port-au-Prince."

Sweet. Unfortunately, the wedding license awaited in St. Thomas, not Haiti.

Speaking of St. Thomas, when I called the wedding planner there, she was nonplussed.

"The weather is gorgeous here," she said. "Tomorrow promises more of the same."

My heart hurt on hearing this. But the captain had taken the *whole* cruise route into account, to avoid rough seas throughout its entirety.

"Surely the cruise line will make things right," another guest said. "Maybe an onboard ceremony, given the change of route?"

Maybe? We'd seen other brides and grooms pose for photos around the ship after exchanging on-ship vows. Just one problem. *Someone* had thrown a hissy fit over the cruise line's wedding services. Chafed at their last-minute puff plans. Demanded a refund.

"I doubt it," I said, something else niggling in the back of my mind.

When I remembered what it was, I felt even worse. I had purchased cruise insurance, yes. But I hadn't purchased wedding insurance, a pesky little incidental that would have guaranteed reimbursement for lost deposits and/or non-refundable payments already made.

Holy cha-ching.

Thankfully, no one grew angry with me or blamed me for messing things up. Still, I stewed in guilt. If only I hadn't cancelled our original plans with the on-line wedding service. Meanwhile, while I pouted, Rice coped by pacing around the ship, 8,000 times. He wouldn't be giving his little girl away after all. Not on this trip.

The younger folks, even Quinn, rebounded quite well. Bummer about the wedding, yes. But the sun shone in Haiti. So, let's party, *mon*. (Ironically, Patrick took it the hardest. "I should be married right now," he lamented at dinner that night.)

I hate to admit it, but Rice and I tucked our respective heads into those places the sun never shines. Sure, we went through the motions, strolling the ship's Central Park before meeting friends and family for dinner. We took Britton to the Boardwalk carousel and snapped his picture enjoying the folded towel animals left by our porter each night. We even managed to chuckle a bit, watching our adult kiddos wipe out on the FlowRider.

In retrospect, we were adrift. We let disappointment block us from savoring so much joy. We missed out on posing for a family group photo or taking in a musical show. We never squished our toes into the sandy beaches or felt the cool aqua waves nip our ankles. While others experienced the thrill of ziplining or hiking the Dunn's River Falls in Ocho Rios, we moped.

Not gonna lie. I regret that we spent our time letting all we had lost choke out the good things, like relishing family, friends, and adventures. I'm grateful our kiddos took pictures and made the best of our calamity at sea. Rice and I didn't take many photos. Certainly, none of ourselves. It's like we knew our sadness and anger would show in our eyes and our posture.

But here's the thing. Today I wish we *did* have a picture that captured all that. Too bad we let ourselves forget: It's not the destination, it's the journey.

In October 2016, Quinn and Patrick *did* get married. In Patrick's parents' backyard. Quinn wore her beautiful ivory-colored dress with the crazy bustle and a delicate veil. I put out the swag I'd planned to share in St. Thomas. Black sunglasses with their original wedding date etched on the side in white ink. Paddle fans that read: "Congrats, Q + P ~ Operation About Damned Time!"

Fortunately, we got tons of pictures this time around. One captures four-year-old Britton, slouched in the sunporch doorway, overwhelmed by all the excitement even before the ceremony began. Another shows Quinn, post-ceremony, twerking for friends by the makeshift bar. (She claims that's untrue and that she was bent over in search of her diamond, momentarily lost when it slipped off her finger.) And then there's one of Rice, wearing Quinn's veil.

There's one more picture worth noting from Quinn and Patrick's reception, one of me, posing in my hot pink mother-of-the-bride gown, wet as a sewer rat. Not an extremely flattering shot, but in my defense, it was Britton's fault.

The kid had finally come out of his funk and was dancing and running around the way four-year-old boys do. I enjoyed watching this but worried that he was getting too close to the edge of the pool. Silly me. As I leaned in to remind him to move a step back...

Oh, yeah. I'm the one who fell into the pool. And I posed for a picture to prove it.

· ♥ ·

Revisiting memories made and lessons learned thus far:

- Favorite wrong turn: Goodbye, St. Thomas; hello, Haiti. Sorry we didn't enjoy you as much as we probably should have.

- Travel tip gleaned: If you're planning a destination wedding, purchase the wedding insurance. Just sayin'.

- Insight into marriage . . . and life: Don't let yourself forget, it's not the destination, it's the journey.

Chapter 18: Love, New England Style

Late 2010s: Rhode Island ~ Maine ~ Vermont

While the Calamity of Errors (aka the wedding cruise) deserved its own chapter, that doesn't mean nothing else happened leading up to it.

The same day Patrick called to ask if he could stop by for Rice's blessings, I received a text message from Alex, just as I was finishing my first cup of morning coffee. The text included a selfie Alex had taken of herself, standing in front of a cute little brick house, keys in hand as she posed beside a SOLD sign.

I practically spit out my drink. *WTH?!?*

"Did *you* know Alex was seriously house hunting?" I asked Rice.

"Not really."

"Me neither." I got up to pour more coffee, remembering back to the mountains of advice we'd sought from my mom when shopping for our first house. "I guess young people these days are less inclined to rely on their older and wiser parents for direction."

Not long after we received Alex's news, a similar thing happened with Daniel. He called to say he and his wife Lauren were relocating from Oklahoma to Rhode Island.

"WTH!?" I actually said it out loud this time.

"Yeah." Daniel chuckled. "Lauren accepted a new job in Providence. Isn't that great?"

After a pause, I said, "I'm very excited for you both!" *Even if you didn't ask our thoughts on this.* "I can't wait to visit."

I meant that, but of course, Rice took it literally and started researching plane flights immediately after their move took place.

"Rhode Island will have to wait," I insisted.

We had just completed the kitchen renovation, and we'd already budgeted time and money to travel for friends' special birthdays and my forty-fifth class reunion. Not to mention, this was shortly before that three-generation cruise, you know, the Calamity of Errors.

"Honey, it can't wait," Rice countered.

"I beg to differ," I said.

In case anyone wonders who wears the pants in our family, I'd like to think we both do. But let me also say this: The next thing I knew, we were on a plane, headed to experience Providence in May.

Yes, sometimes I fret that these adult kiddos of ours are going to be the death of me. Whenever that happens, I repeat the new mantra I'm still trying to embrace:

It's their story now.

And P.S. They're going to carry it out with their own style and on their own timeline.

· ♥ ·

Daniel and Lauren's white clapboard duplex lay on the East Side of town close to Brown University. Victorian homes and impeccably landscaped yards lined their neighborhood. Sometimes we'd sit out on their second-story balcony and people-watch over cocktails. A youthful vibe and energy wafted up from the street.

We did a lot of walking, in the residential area as well as the shopping area down near Tortilla Flats. Daniel and Lauren loved to bring Winston, their corgi, along for the fun as we strolled shops selling items ranging from rustic yard art to freshly butchered meats. Blooms spilled from hanging pots near the River, and the breeze picked up their scent. Winston waggled along, happy for attention from other dogs and Corgi lovers. (The latter are a cult, y'all.)

Speaking of cults, believe it or not, reminds me of donuts. Yes, donuts. Folks in the South *insist* that Krispy Kremes rule when it comes to donuts. I've lived in Georgia for over thirty years, and, respectfully, I beg to differ. Hands down, nothing beats a good ol' up-north cake donut. And Rhode Island donuts, especially Allie's Donuts in North Kingstown, did not disappoint. We tried other local delicacies, too, like coffee milk. (Meh.) And how could we not stop for a Coney Island hotdog at Olneyville New York System?

One day during our visit, Daniel drove us to Newport, where we ogled the multi-million-dollar homes for sale along the crystal-clear waterfront. Taking in all that secondhand wealth built up an appetite, so we stopped for a bite, and I tried my first lobster roll, a hot one covered in melted butter. One word: OMG.

Amid all the craziness and activity of 2016, I'm so glad we visited Providence that May . . . Because, like many young couples building careers, Daniel and Lauren relocated again not too long after our visit.

On the downside, that meant no more visits to Providence.

On the upside, we see them more often these days. Their next relocation was to Atlanta.

· ♥ ·

Flash forward to fall 2018. Rice and I sat in the Delta Sky Club at Atlanta's Hartsfield-Jackson International Airport, sipping wine before a flight to Portland International Jetport. We somehow got to chatting with a couple of women, one married to an Episcopal bishop. The women had just visited Plains, Georgia, to check off a bucket-list item, visiting Jimmy and Rosalyn Carter's Sunday School class. During this same Sky Club visit, we also met a gentleman who'd grown up in Poland during the Holocaust. He spent a huge part of his youth hiding out in a basement. Now he was seeing the world with Wife Number Two, a visionary and yoga coach.

Our destination for this trip was one from *my* bucket list, a place I'd seen on the old TV show, *Murder, She Wrote*. It featured an author "of age," J.B. (Jessica) Fletcher, who wrote and solved murder mysteries from her home in quaint Cabot Cove, Maine. Granted, the murder-to-resident ratio there was abysmal. And it was fictional. Still, I wanted to visit.

Our first stop was Ogunquit, where we hiked the Marginal Way, a paved path alongside the ocean. It's a fairly easy trek with benches along the path for resting, flowers and cairns and a lighthouse to ogle, and the sea, breaking its salty waves against rocks and sand.

We stayed at a bed and breakfast in Kennebunk that first night. We feasted on blueberry pancakes with coconut blueberry butter and a poached pear. Our host said in winter, the town turns into a Hallmark holiday movie set. I found it charming already, its Main Street flanking a waterfront moored with sailboats and fishing skiffs. Yup. My own private Cabot Cove.

After breakfast, we drove to Mt. Battie, where fog blocked its usually panoramic view. From there, we somehow discovered the sweeping grounds and gardens of St. Anthony's Monastery. It's a beautiful Franciscan Friary that boasts stone statues and sculpted angels and a hermitage that looked like a Tudor-style house. Another off-the-beaten path delight.

Back on the road, we passed through small towns lined with clapboard houses, their yards lush with giant orange pumpkins and dense clumps of crimson ivy. We stayed at another quaint B&B, this one in Camden. It served another sumptuous breakfast, watermelon and kiwi with coconut lime cream, followed by eggs Florentine and black pepper candied bacon. Feeling a bit too fat and happy, we drove on to Rockland, where we hiked up to see Owl's Head Light House perched above the sparkling Penobscot Bay.

From Rockland, we took to the road in search of local distilleries and wineries. Listen, I *do* like to taste the wares, but it's more than that. Really. Vineyards and wineries provide peaceful settings, lush and natural, and they frequently host live music.

In Union, the wines were good, the music mellow, the settings natural. At one stop, free-range chickens strutted the grounds, pecking for grubs at their feet. At another, we saw our first belted Galloway cow, a solid black cow from head to toe, except for a band of white around its belly. They're affectionately called "Oreo cows." Because that's what they look like, I kid you not.

Back on the road, a llama pack grazed behind a fence so close I could almost touch them.

"Pull over!" I hollered to Rice.

He did, but without ever braking. My heart lurched along with the car. Thank goodness I didn't wet myself, hearing the screech of tires skidding on gravel as the car stopped. As for the llamas, I captured one's expression in a photo. It looks like she's saying: "WTH?!?"

After apologizing profusely to the llamas, we hit Bar Harbor, ate lunch at the Thirsty Whale, then checked into B&B Number Three. Our hosts, two elderly gents, told us in kind but unconditional tones that we'd have to lug our own suitcases up to our third-floor room. Ugh. We transferred necessities from our trunk into canvas grocery bags and toted them up the stairs.

Our hosts redeemed themselves later, directing us to walk down a winding road into town and to Beall's, a pick-your-own lobster place on the water. I brushed away guilty thoughts of lobsters screaming in boiling water and chose my 1.66-pound dinner. We ate off paper plates at a community table while chatting with a couple from Colorado. This was exactly how I'd pictured Maine would be.

We encountered more fog—again—the next day, thwarting our view of Mt. Cadillac. We visited anyway, sharing an over-hyped "popover" at Jordan's Pond and hiking the Wild Gardens of Acadia. (I fell in love with the massive rusty-orange ferns there). My favorite stop along Park Loop Road may have been Thunder Hole, where rocks tower over a tiny inlet. An hour before high tide, waves gush in, frantic and wild, forcing the air trapped in the rocks' chasm back out in a massive, thunder-like crash. I don't really understand the science, but it awed me.

Book nerd that I am, I asked Rice to drive from Bar Harbor to Bangor to check out a spot I *thought* might be Stephen King's house. We weren't the only tourists to stop for a gawk at a towering red house with white trim. It sat behind a wrought-iron fence, embellished with bats and spiders and a three-headed reptile.

We made one more stop, this one for Rice, because of his love of history and geography.

Portsmouth, New Hampshire, sits on the Piscataqua River, small and mighty. It charmed us both, especially Market Square, where teens dressed in Revolutionary garb played songs on fifes from the days of Colonial America. It was lovely but too short a stop.

Smitten by New England, we both hoped to return. It was only a matter of when.

· ♥ ·

Less than a year later, we flew to Vermont to celebrate forty years of marriage in July 2019. New England's small towns on seaports had beckoned us back. Its stone hedges and country stores, as well as its down-to-earth people, lent to its alure.

Our first afternoon, we set out to see Lake Champlain. Driving around it, we came across the colorful Birdhouse Forest, where over 400 birdhouses, painted in striking bright colors, line the woods. Tucked in among the birdhouses, massive metal sculpted dinosaurs peered our way. I felt like an awestruck child, letting the wind whip my hair through the open car window, discovering fun surprises at every turn.

After the Birdhouse Forest, the fairytale drive continued. For several miles, we scanned the roadside for miniature medieval castles. Dozens of them, maybe waist-high, sat nestled within the landscape of people's private yards. Built by a Swiss emigrant in the 1920s, these structures have meticulously stacked stone and glazed windows. Some are surrounded by moats. A few have been rigged with running water and electricity.

Respectful of people's property, we stopped on occasion to photograph some of the castles from a short distance. During one stop, we heard music. Barenaked Ladies' "If I Had $1,000,000" wafted from speakers over a sprawling lawn up the road. It came from a vineyard, hosting an after-party for some sort of bicycle tour or race. It lent another layer of richness to an already splendid day.

Back in Burlington, we wound down with wine and cheese by the hotel pool. We tried not to eavesdrop on a couple nearby, but she was loud, prattling on ad nauseam. The man only made a guttural noise now and then. A sign he was listening? Or just an effort to stay awake.

"What a horrible first date," I murmured to Rice.

He randomly picked up a piece of cheese, then looked at me, puzzled, as though I'd said something odd.

"She's so boring," I explained. "If she keeps rambling on, there won't be a second date. I can guarantee it."

At that point, Rice broke a smile. "Honey, who would bring a first date to a hotel?"

He laughed as I looked toward the couple, whose dynamics hadn't changed.

"You have a point, I'll give you that," I said. After another quick glance in the couple's direction, I added, "But still, I stand by my theory."

We never did learn the couple's story. It wasn't our business, after all. But watching them reminded me that it had been decades since our first date, back when we started testing the waters . . . looking for mutual interests . . . taking a pulse to find connections beyond just the physical draw. I squeezed Rice's hand, grateful those days were behind us.

· ♥ ·

For our fortieth anniversary meal, we ate at an outside cafe on the Burlington pedestrian mall. A soothing breeze made the small colorful lights strewn in the trees twinkle. It reminded me so much of Boulder.

"Remember our first anniversary?" Rice said, apparently on the same wavelength.

I nodded. "You took me to dinner at John's." And I had found the French menu too fancy, the prices too steep.

He smirked. "Not my best pick of all times."

"Are you kidding?" I wrinkled my forehead. "You were trying to up our game. And I'd say it worked," I added. "I mean, look at us now."

We sat, coupled in silence, sharing our bond through a graze of hands and a smile.

Over the next couple days, we took a few side trips, walking through sculpture gardens of children and animals in Stowe, hiking tree-lined paths past gushing waterfalls in Woodstock. When mom-and-pop stores called our names, we listened, stopping along the way to try cider donuts and just about anything maple, most notably ice cream, but also martinis.

Not sure why, but this trip left us both a bit camera crazy. I credit (or blame) Vermont for my new-found fetish to photograph murals. *All* the murals. Meanwhile, Rice focused on taking photos of landscapes and lingering shots of the sun as it rose and set over Lake Champlain. We both developed a crazy crush on capturing pictures of old mills and covered bridges. In one of my favorites, Rice got a shot of Jericho's Old Red Mill, tiger lilies bent in the breeze on its left, river waters churning downstream on its right.

Back home, I framed Rice's picture of Jericho's Old Red Mill for a space above the tub in our master bath. Above it I hung a shot from Ogunquit.

Later that week, I enlarged some Italy shots for above the family room sofa. It's as if I knew how long those memories would have to sustain us.

I didn't, of course. None of us did.

Who would have guessed that a few months later, we'd find ourselves under a bona fide quarantine? Who would have guessed the world, as we knew it, would never again be the same?

· ♥ ·

Revisiting memories made and lessons learned thus far:

- Favorite wrong turn: Rice changed hotel reservations for our last night in Maine—at my request, to save some money. He managed to book us into another Hilton property in Portland. Portland, Oregon, that is. Not Portland, Maine.

- Travel tip gleaned: Travel while you're able and when the opportunity arises. Seriously.

- Insight into marriage . . . and life: When the kiddos become adults, repeat these words after me: "It's their story now."

PART IV: At the Round-About, Take the Road Not Yet Traveled

Chapter 19: Exploring Along the Eastern Seaboard

2020-2021: The Carolinas ~ Maryland ~ Virginia

J anuary 1, 2020, marked my first official day of retirement. Rice's was scheduled for April 1st. No foolin'. I opted to pass on a big retirement to-do, but Rice was stoked for his. And he also started to muse about getting back to Europe. Soon.

With retirement under my belt—and before Rice could whisk me off on a trip—I started a six-week novel revision workshop with author Joshilyn Jackson through the Decatur Writers Studio. Ten of us gathered with her at Decatur CoWorks each week. After class, we'd move to Las Brasas, a Peruvian restaurant next door, where we'd nosh and dish more with Joss about the publishing industry and the writing community. I savored this new focus—on building a more creative life.

Then came the Ides of March, when our in-person classes got cancelled. We chafed when the class went virtual, but at least we all learned how to Zoom. We'd return to Las Brasas eventually, but only in splintered subgroups, and not until well over a year had gone by.

Late March brought lockdown. Rice's retirement party got canceled. Our plans for Europe got blurred. I received texts from former co-workers, still working in public health:

"We're working overtime, six days a week, no leave, no flex . . ."
"Please pray for us . . ."

"All I want to do is sleep . . . " "It is hard to sleep. I keep waking up in a panic . . ."

Their messages made my heart ache for them. Yet I also felt selfish relief. I wasn't having to crank out grant applications ad nauseam to beg for emergency funds. My worst days now involved canceled plans. Or needing to use sub-par toilet paper. On my lousiest days, I never experienced having to put myself at risk. So, yes, I felt guilty. Very much so.

That summer, kids' camps got canceled, and open swim at the neighborhood pool gave way to a sign-up system of staggering times to allow social distancing. By fall, our third-grade grandson attended school full-time via Zoom. While his parents reported to work, Britton reported to JJ and Big Daddy's house, or to his Nana's, to pursue his remote education. I'm embarrassed to say, my joy as a grandparent diminished some then. Rice's, too, I think. (He's too kind to admit it, though.)

Rice had told people that in his retirement, he planned to live out his lifelong dream of raising llamas. Instead, he continued his gig as school monitor, P.E. teacher, bus driver, and third-grade lunch lady. Meanwhile, I focused on writing as best as I could.

Finally, in October, schools resumed in person, and with caution, Rice and I ventured back out into the world. We started with visits to nearby vineyards to chill over wine and enjoy live music. We expanded our reach with a birthday weekend in Clarksville, Georgia, where we sipped prosecco beside the pool and enjoyed farm-to-table meals at the Glen-Ella Springs Inn. Even after a storm wiped out the inn's power, the owners served a delicious hot breakfast by lantern light—and with the help of a very hearty generator.

By December, I was more than tired of all the precautions and social distancing. A vaccine had yet to be approved, but surely a family holiday gathering would be okay.

"Christmas dinner at our house this year!" I decided for everyone. "No excuses!"

But being the Rices (the senior Rices, at that), on Christmas Eve Day, we learned that we'd been exposed to COVID. We canceled original plans and bided our time Christmas Day in an Urgent Care waiting room. Thankfully, our test results came back negative. We celebrated our Christmas in January. I got a family photo and sent out Valentine greetings in lieu of Christmas or New Year's cards.

Post pandemic, I've tried to be grateful. Our immediate family came through okay, our health and our lifestyles mostly unscathed. Globally, we learned new skills and how to appreciate what we have. Some of us even learned to bake sourdough. Others acquired new pets to love.

On my best days, I'd say the pandemic reminded us all that we are one people.

Yet sometimes—not often, but sometimes—my thoughts run darker. Those are the days I fret that we'll never fully recover all that we lost.

· ♥ ·

By June 2021, Rice and I had each received two vaccines. Air travel still felt more daunting than road trips, which got us thinking: How many United States had we already visited? Turns out the answer was forty-two. We had not yet seen Utah, New Mexico, Idaho, or Connecticut. Also on our still-to-come list: Montana, the two Dakotas, and Alaska.

If we focused on U.S. travel and visited two or three new states each year, we could reach fifty states, maybe by 2024.

Before tackling our Fifty-State Project, we wanted to see family that we'd been missing. That's why our first post-pandemic road trip of any distance was to see my sister Lynne, who'd moved to the Baltimore area.

Opting to hug the Eastern seaboard on our way north, we set out. No new states for this trek, but plenty of new places and things to see.

The beauty of water has always captivated me, more so oceans and lakes than brackish swamps and marshes. Still, I was struck by a haunting beauty in the South Carolina marshlands. Silver-gray tree trunks protruded, naked and dead. The landscape was eerie and exquisite. But sad. Climate change was killing these trees. These rotting ghost forests would never regenerate.

On a more positive note, we stopped for the night in Wilmington, North Carolina, a small town with a big New Orleans flair. Its Riverwalk beckoned, and after strolling that, we roamed further into town, where quite a few wrought iron balconies overlooked the quaint streets.

The next day we drove to New Bern to seek out life-sized fiberglass sculptures of bears. Local artists had painted dozens of these to honor the town's 300th birthday in 2010. We had fun looking for the colorful structures. (Who says adults can't enjoy scavenger hunts, eh?)

Even stifling heat didn't detract from New Bern's beauty. We discovered alleyways lined with benches and sparkling white lights. In an Episcopal Churchyard, Spanish moss hung from trees, framing old gravestones so mottled with age that we couldn't read what they said.

We took a detour on our way out of North Carolina, hoping to see the Wright Brothers National Memorial in Kitty Hawk. Who knew it had visiting hours? We only learned that as we drove by, and a flashing sign read: "Sorry you missed us today. Come back tomorrow."

Disappointed, we drove on, and smack-dab straight into a speed trap. The ticket was bummer enough, but it came with a bonus. North Carolina had recently mandated in-person court appearances, meaning we had a choice: (1) drive eight-plus hours from home to North Carolina to make the mandatory court appearance, or (2) pay a lawyer to make said appearance. For me.

Yes, it was me. Damned my lead foot. Thirteen letters from North Carolina lawyers, soliciting my business, awaited me on my return to Atlanta. No worries, though. Three hundred sixty-five dollars later, all was well.

I vowed to use cruise control moving forward and then turned my worries to whether driving the seventeen-mile Chesapeake Bay Bridge Tunnel might bother landlubber Rice. Funny enough, the thought of maneuvering a car in a tunnel under sections of ocean troubled him less than it did me. He drove the tunnel just fine to get us to Virginia's Chincoteague Island, where I'd hoped to see the wild ponies. Come to find out, we were visiting off-season. Of course.

Back on the road, we detoured to see Rehoboth Beach, the Bidens' favorite Delaware getaway. We caught nary a glimpse of Joe or Jill. Perhaps they had visiting hours too?

No complaints, though. We'd breezed in and out of three states in less than a day.

When we finally reached Bel Air, Maryland, I fell in love with yet another small town. Our first morning there, I sipped steaming coffee from Lynne and her husband Kim's balcony porch and admired a family of deer by a stream in their backyard.

"I can understand why Lynne and Kim love it here," I murmured to Rice.

"Don't even think it!" he said, raising his eyebrows.

(You might recall, Lynne and Kim originally lured us to Georgia. We had lived seven miles apart for thirty years, until they followed their daughter north to Bel Air.)

In downtown Bel Air, we checked out shops in eighteenth century buildings as well as large Gothic Revival-style churches tucked among the trees. Walking the town took us by a restaurant with rooftop dining, a town fountain, and lots of government buildings. Pink petunias hung from wrought iron posts, and a barber shop displayed an old-fashioned pole of red, white, and blue helix stripes.

From downtown, we drove to Tudor Hall, the home of John Wilkes Booth when he was a boy. It operates as a museum these days. Rice, who loves all things Abraham Lincoln-related, was psyched to visit. So was Kim, an avid history buff himself. We followed the GPS to the address we'd found online, which took us into a quiet residential section of the town.

"Is this it?" Lynne asked.

"I think so," Rice said, putting the car in park and hopping out to get a better glimpse of a nearby sign.

When he turned back toward us, his posture told us all we needed to know.

"We're at the right place," he said once back in the car. "But it's only open a couple Sundays and Mondays each month,"

Hot damn. Once again, we'd arrived a day late and a dollar short.

We pivoted with a side trip to Havre de Grace, another pretty suburban town where Lynne and Kim now shop for mid-century modern décor instead of their one-time beloved antiques.

Our visit included a day trip to St. Michaels, a maritime town where we picked up a piece of anniversary cake, a colorful version of Maryland's signature Smith Island cake—six layers of feathery yellow cake topped with a schmear of chocolate icing. We got the cake to go in honor of Lynne and Kim's fifty-two years of marriage. We toasted them over the best crab cakes ever at a place called Box Hill Pizzeria and Crabcakes in Bel Air. Go figure.

Once on our way back to Atlanta, a couple more spots called out to us, starting with Frederick, Maryland, which some call a place with small city charm and a big city pulse. After a very brief visit, I concur. Our morning stop prohibited exploring along the Frederick Wine Trail. Instead, we wandered downtown, along the pedestrian walkway that edges against Carroll Creek Park. We strolled beside the creek, enjoying the Delaplaine sculpture garden and the colorful work displayed on the creek's massive stone moon bridge.

Next, we stopped in Harpers Ferry, West Virginia, the spot of John Brown's ill-fated raid The town's rustic buildings brimmed over with history and old-town ambiance. Looking out over the valley from the edge of town provided a stunning view. It helped spur us back to our journey, driving lush back roads to I-81, breathing in mountain beauty along the Shenandoah Valley, and finally winding our way to Roanoke, Virginia.

Roanoke proved to be so much more than just a convenient overnight stop along the route. In some ways, it was just one more walkable city with hibiscus, begonias, and vines brimming from flower boxes along the streets. One more place to play tacky tourist, buying wine glasses from Well Hung Vineyard, then taking night photos of Rice jumping in and out of the fountain near our hotel. Sometimes a place just clicks. For both of us and for reasons we can't explain.

We met a loquacious beat cop making his rounds near our hotel the next morning.

"Anywhere good for breakfast?" Rice asked.

"Plenty of places," the officer said. "But first tell me what you like to eat."

He kept on talking, never giving us a chance to respond.

"Personally, I'm into keto." He talked up the wonders of keto and water, then talked about it some more. Finally, he steered us toward the locally owned Ernie's for breakfast.

"Is it keto-friendly?" I asked Rice as we neared it.

"It must be . . ." he said.

". . . if Officer Swisher recommended it." We said that last part in unison.

Laughing, we made our way into Ernie's, which, sure enough, offered a wide variety of breakfast items We could eat keto-friendly if we chose to do so. But who could resist the aroma of crisply cooked bacon and biscuits, served piping hot?

After we left Ernie's, we walked along Market Square, where vendors were setting up shop for the morning. Still going strong today, Roanoke's Farmer's Market began in 1882. It's considered the oldest open-air market in Virginia. As we walked, I noticed a porcelain mosaic underfoot of an Italian mama serving up pasta. I snapped a picture. I would enhance my new mural collection by adding a mosaic every now and then.

Before leaving town, on a fluke, we drove up to Mill Mountain Park, where the Roanoke Star overlooks the city. We hiked an amazing wildflower garden filled with local ferns and flowers and gooseneck loosestrife. It led to a quaint little petting zoo, which reminded me I missed my grands.

Even so, I hated to leave.

As Rice began the drive home, I dozed. When he tapped my arm, my eyes fluttered open. He nodded toward a sign on my side of the road.

I read it out loud. "Virginia is for Lovers."

He didn't utter a word—just looked at me and grinned.

I returned his smile. Then I closed my eyes again, ready to dream of being back home again with my love . . . grateful for one more adventure under our belt, hopeful for more smooth roads still to come.

· ♥ ·

Revisiting memories made and lessons learned thus far:

- Favorite wrong turn: Discovering the wildflower garden and petting zoo atop Mill Mountain Park.

- Travel tip gleaned: Setting the cruise control for seven miles over the limit won't win you the Indy. But it might save you money and keep you safe.

- Insight into marriage . . . and life: When you find a place that clicks for both of you, don't overthink it or try to pinpoint why. Just go for it, baby. Go for it!

Chapter 20: In the Air Again ~ Off to the Cowboy, Salt Lake & Gem States

2021: Wyoming ~ Idaho ~ Utah

B uoyed by our road trip of summer 2021, we discussed hitting the skies—and new states—that fall.

"Where do you want to go next?" Rice asked.

I thought for a minute, then said, "Let's do Idaho?"

He lifted a brow. "Idaho?"

"Hey, you like potatoes," I ribbed him. "Plus, my Aunt Pat's there, and it's one of the eight states we still haven't seen."

We priced round-trip flights from Atlanta to Boise. *Yikes.* Changing plans probably cost us even more, but we opted to fly into Denver as a starting point and revisit old friends from the place and time we'd started our life together—Colorado. That would mean driving from Colorado through Wyoming to get to Idaho. But . . . if we drove down to Salt Lake and then flew home from there, we'd have *two* more new states under our belts, Idaho and Utah.

Mere days before our trip, COVID's Delta variant hit. I panicked. Two of the six people we planned to visit were octogenarians. Rice and I thought it only fair to reach out to say we were vaxed, but if they wanted to take a raincheck for safety's sake, we'd understand. One of the younger couples replied: "We're still good to meet. But just FYI, we have elected NOT to vax."

That surprised us. We struggled with what to do. In the end, though, we planned a Zoom visit with them instead of getting together face to face. For safety's sake.

Boulder had changed. We barely recognized Pearl Street Mall. God love the falafel place. It remained open, as did my favorite, Pasta Jay's. (Its Baked Lorenzo is amazing.) And examples of Boulder's love-is-love, tree-hugging vibe lived on, through rainbow-lined crosswalks and three-bucket waste stops, labeled: Recycle – Landfill – and (wait for it . . .) – Compost.

Out in Gunbarrel Estates, we drove down our old residential street and slowed to see Timmy, our first house. Amazingly, he was still yellow. The trees we'd planted to celebrate each child's birth now blocked the view of the Flatirons we once enjoyed from the patio. I pondered if the view might be better out back. When Rice didn't stop me, I knocked on the door, seeking permission to walk in the yard to get a better look.

The new owner—let's call her D—said, "Of course!"

Out back, up near the house, she'd replaced the patio we'd installed, repurposing its bricks to frame flower beds down by the fence. I breathed in the grass and enjoyed the sun on my back as the memories gushed over. Rice, building a rustic sandbox from wood . . . or ridding the garden tomatoes of hornworms so big they made me scream. Grilling on the brick patio. Wicked croquet games after we ate. Me, eight months pregnant with Quinn (and huge!), chasing down Alex and friends at her fourth birthday party. All for the love of Duck-Duck-Goose.

"Do you want to come inside?" D's question jolted me back to the present.

She led us into the dining room, which provided a full peek into the living room. Everything seemed so much smaller than I recalled.

"Want to see the basement?" she asked.

Her offer surprised both Rice and me. So did how little the basement had changed. It still had the same dark paneling we had put up and oatmeal-hued carpet we had installed. It was a mess though, with piles of items stashed along all the walls and in the corners. D, dare I say, appeared to be a hoarder.

It hurt some to see that the great room we'd lived in so long ago now served as a storage facility. But like they say: *You can't go home again.*

I think Rice might even add: *And you shouldn't.* Being a nice guy, he carried a fifty-pound bag of dog food down the stairs. What could he say when D asked, "Do you mind?" He also helped hang a shower curtain in the basement bathroom, but that one's on me. D was struggling with the curtain while showing us the bathroom she'd put in, and I blurted out, "Help her, Rice!"

Oh, Rice . . .

Before leaving Boulder, we met up with Kate and Jerry, the kind of friends you wish you never had to leave behind. They hadn't changed, but some other things had. We learned an old boss of Rice's had died from COVID. And we discovered a marijuana dispensary, StarBuds, out near the health club we used to visit.

In Fort Collins, we visited dear friends Hugh and Helen, who served us beer and ribs at their Santa Fe-style home. They drove us around Horsetooth Reservoir and then into Old Town for drinks at Sunny Lubrick's. We left Colorado, filled with good food and warm memories, the aspen twinkling behind us in golden glory.

· ♥ ·

Antelope grazed the plains along U.S. 287 in Wyoming. The road stretched so far and wide we could almost see forever. Rice didn't even squawk when I drove eighty miles per hour. (Although come to think of it, maybe that's actually the speed limit there.)

Our drive took us past the University of Wyoming's Laramie campus, then on to the Territorial Prison, where Butch Cassidy once served time. We lunched at a hole-in-the-wall Mexican restaurant, then crossed the Continental Divide. Along the way, cowboys on horseback drove large herds of cattle, kicking up dust and tumbleweeds in the process. Despite some interesting cowboy sightings, we had known that the drive through Wyoming would drain us. Sure enough, we were pooped by the time we reached Rock Springs. We lugged our bags into the hotel, ready to clean up and go out for dinner. Yet after several attempts to get into the room, Rice couldn't do it.

"Wait here," he said. And with much irritation, he went to the lobby to complain.

He wasn't gone long before he came back, wearing a sheepish expression.

"What's wrong?" I asked.

"I told the front desk that my contactless check-in was not letting me in the room."

"Okay? And . . . ?"

"Well . . ." An embarrassed smile started to break through. "The clerk looked at my iPhone and bit her lip. Then she said, 'Sir, it looks like you reserved a room at the Homewood Suites. This is the Hampton Inn.'"
Oh, Rice...

By the time we toted our bags back downstairs and past the lobby, even he saw the humor in things.

"I'll be sure to give you a five-star review," he assured the Hampton staff as we left.

We crossed into Utah on I-80, then followed I-15 North into Idaho. Destination: Buhl, a small town that's known as the Trout Capital of the

World. My Aunt Pat lived there, along with my cousin, Beth, who had invited us to visit.

In many ways, Beth and I were strangers. My father died when I was a toddler, and I lost close contact with most of his family, the Putnams. Beth had reached out to me several years earlier, when she and her husband, Sam, had an Atlanta layover.

"Can we stop by to visit?" she asked.

God love Beth. She's never met a stranger, a fact that brought us to Buhl, where Sam and Beth had just bought a house in Snake River Canyon. The minute we stepped into their house, it felt like a step back in time. The seventies, to be specific. This déjà vu possibly came from the scent of adult recreational herbal treats. Used in abundance. And with no hesitancy to share.

"So why Buhl?" Rice asked, once we had settled in and relaxed for a bit.

Beth smiled. "I get visions . . . in the mornings, led by the spirits. First, they guided me to the City of Lights. Then to the Snake River Canyon."

Oh . . . Was she implying she was a seer? Or a witch?

Whether she was or wasn't, the logistics tracked. Sam and Beth had lived in Phoenix for years. From there they moved to Las Vegas, a "City of Lights." Now they had come to the Snake River Canyon and brought along Beth's mom, Pat, a spunky, spry widow just shy of eighty.

Pat had married Keith, my dad's brother, and I was hoping to hear stories about the father I never knew. Pat hadn't known him well either, as he passed away shortly after she and Keith married. Still, I'm so glad I got to spend time with her. She's passed on since our visit, but Pat was as warm as Beth and made me feel like, well, part of the family.

Rice too. He told me later: "Everyone should have an Aunt Pat."

As for Sam and Beth, they're kind and big-hearted and march to their own drum. Do we believe Beth gets visions? Who knows? I believe *she* believes she does, and that's enough for me. Unless folks present a danger to others, I tend to say let's live and let live.

During our visit, Sam drove us along the Snake River, surrounded by vast rolling plains. He wove past historic old barns and a farm with a zebra and camels. He dropped us at trailheads that led to short hikes to the churning Shoshone Falls and Niagara Springs. Later, we grabbed a beer at the West Point Bar—a hole in the wall with outstanding Halloween décor. (Loved the cobweb-shrouded skeleton, posed at a piano mid-song.) We also checked out Magic Valley Brewing, where the Paintbrush dark ale was a favorite, hands down.

Beside the lush views of the river and valley, one of the loveliest things at Beth and Sam's place was their garden. I lusted over that screened-in structure that Sam had constructed, with help from a friend and a YouTube tutorial. Time in the garden with Beth, tending and harvesting plants, made me want to expand my own garden back home. (And, no, I didn't see any special herbs growing beyond the kinds you can buy at your local grocer's.)

On the last night of our visit, Beth handled food prep and Sam grilled. We enjoyed steaks with leek cream sauce and a salad of home-grown greens and vegetables. For dessert, we all made our own s'mores with Ghirardelli dark caramel chocolate. *Yum.*

So . . . maybe Beth *is* a witch. She sure knew how to make magic in the kitchen!

We ended our trip in Salt Lake City, Utah, where the manager's reception at the hotel was dry and the Tabernacle lay under cover, mid-renovations. Rice smashed his finger in a door, and we discovered the Great Salt Lake lay more than a dozen miles from town. Its water was low. I'd heard that this lake, the largest salt lake in the Western hemisphere, was drying up. Still, I wasn't ready for what I saw—a bleak expanse of salty sand that stretched for miles. What a shame for the environment, but also for Utah's economy and public health system.

On a more positive note, our drive through Park City was gorgeous—hilly terrain, vibrant leaves, funky shops, crisp air. My kind of place, for sure.

We probably need to return to the Beehive State one more time just to do it justice. We missed seeing so many places, like Bryce Canyon, Powell Lake, and Monument Valley. And I've heard Moab is stunning.

Sigh. There are so many places we'd like to visit again. But first, we needed to finish our Fifty-State Project.

· ❤ ·

Revisiting memories made and lessons learned thus far:

- Favorite wrong turn: Our stop at the Hampton Inn in Rock Springs, Wyoming.

- Travel tip gleaned: Remember not to beat yourself up when you don't see it all. You simply can't. And that's okay.

- Insight into marriage . . . and life: If we're lucky, we meet special people along life's journey. If we're extra lucky, some of those people remain on our journey for more than one stop.

Chapter 21: State No. Forty-Five For Us ~ The Land of Enchantment

2022: New Mexico

It's funny the silly preconceptions we carry when we set out to explore a new destination. For instance, I worried I wouldn't like Taos because a friend once told me it smelled like urine. In February 2022, when we rented a car in Albuquerque, I mentally prepared myself for that as well as for driving through miles and miles of open ocher landscape to get to Santa Fe.

I needn't have worried. The colors and diverse beauty of New Mexico took my breath away, starting with its crystal blue skies. The desert landscape did spread before us in a tawny rocky mass, but it was also kissed by touches of gray and white and adobe pink.

The most direct driving route from Albuquerque to Santa Fe is along I-25. We didn't take that. Instead, we followed the Turquoise Trail, a longer but more scenic route between the two cities. I'd read about it on Pinterest. (In addition to Foder and Frommer and Rick Steves, I sometimes use Pinterest when planning our travels.)

According to Pinterest, we should look for a quarter-mile section of Route 66 near Tijeras. It contained rumble strips that, if crossed at just the right speed, would play "America the Beautiful." After a few false starts, we finally saw a sign for the Musical Highway.

"I *think* I hear the song," I told Rice, after he made several attempts to drive over the rumble strips.

"And I think you're imagining things," he scoffed.

"Well," I shot back, "you're not driving exactly forty-five miles per hour. Maybe that's why we can't hear the music the way we should."

We huffed a little more at each other but agreed to move on, even though we never did hear "America the Beautiful." Only later would we learn that the Musical Highway, built in 2014 to get folks to slow down, fell into disarray in 2020. No current plans exist to bring it back to its glory.

Undeterred, we continued the Turquoise Trail, along winding roads that passed mining towns and artist communities. Rice skidded to a stop near Golden when I spotted a colorful junk yard sign and hollered, "Pull over!" He did, and we discovered a mix of folk art and hubcaps and dried herbs for sale.

We made another stop a little down the highway in Madrid. We walked an area of town to discover some local eateries and art galleries and a radio station, KMRD 96.9 FM. People ambled the streets at a leisurely pace, many with dogs in tow. We ate at the Holler, which featured fried green tomatoes on special, but also offered a Howler menu with items like doggie veggie nachos and homemade milk bones.

By the time we reached Santa Fe, we were pooped, and *someone* was on the verge of hanger. When we pulled into the parking lot of the Old Santa Fe Inn, I tried to mask my disappointment. The exterior of the place resembled an old Howard Johnson motor lodge, thankfully sans the orange and turquoise trim.

We dumped off our bags in the room and decided to walk to a nearby restaurant we'd read about. I entered its name into my phone's GPS system, and we walked. As we neared the end of our route, I glanced at my phone, which now flickered. *Damn.* I swear we'd been a mere tenth of a mile away, but now the GPS showed we still had eight-tenths of a mile to go.

So, we walked and walked some more. Just when it looked like we were less than a tenth of a mile from the restaurant (again), the map on my phone flickered (again). The screen flipped around ad nauseam, and suddenly it showed (again) that we had eight-tenths of a mile to go.

"What's the deal?" I stuck my phone under Rice's face. "Where the hell *is* this place?"

He plucked the phone from my hand and gave it a long stare. His lips twitched.

Finally, he handed it back to me. "In the future," he said, "when we're not driving, you might want to reset your GPS to the walk mode."

We ate somewhere else that first night, and after a good night's sleep—with our window open in February!—we discovered, to our surprise, that we loved the Old Santa Fe Inn. Our room had a Kiva-style fireplace, which we lit after visiting the free breakfast burrito bar next door. Now refreshed, I noticed clusters of dried red chilis and hanging flower baskets adorning the inn's exterior. Inside, we shared a sitting alcove with two other guest rooms. Cheerful daylight streamed through the floor-to-ceiling window that ran its full length. The two other rooms remained vacant, so the alcove became my own private makeup and sitting area throughout our stay. I loved it.

One morning we woke up to several inches of snow. I behaved like a giddy little girl, dancing in the glittery white stuff that now graced the Plaza of our nation's oldest capital city. Rice was a good sport, given how much he's come to dislike the cold. We visited a couple trading posts in search of gifts to take home to the grands.

Another day, after the snow had melted, we visited Santa Fe's farmers market in the Railyard District. After that, we drove along Canyon Road to gape at the contemporary outdoor sculptures. We also stopped by the

International Folk Art Museum, which features hundreds of miniature displays of communities throughout the world. One of my favorites showcased an Asian couple in a colorful wedding rickshaw, celebrating their new life together. The creepiest had to be the miniature plague doctor, clad in gloves and boots and a long, protective coat, topped with a black hat that perched above an ominous long-beaked bird mask.

For someone who doesn't gravitate toward museums, I found the place fascinating. And I learned that those bird masks were packed with spices, herbs, and dried flowers in hopes of keeping the doctors safe during the Plague of 1656.

We didn't reserve tickets in time to visit the Georgia O'Keeffe Museum, so instead we drove to the place she spent her final years. From the interstate, we could see snowcapped mountain peaks jutting up into open blue skies. As we ventured off the highway closer to Abiquiú, we encountered dusty rolling back roads where tumbleweeds nipped at our bumper. We saw loads of adobe. And livestock. New Mexico has more livestock than people.

Incredible stone landscape surrounded us. Some of it was, uh, quite phallic. We took pictures at the Santa Rosa de Linda Ruins, the Abiquiú Library, and the Santo Tomas El Apostal church. We think we found Georgia O'Keeffe's modest old home, but who can be sure?

From Abiquiú we visited Ghost Ranch on one of the prettiest drives of the trip. We drank in the clean air and the breathtaking views of red and yellow sandstone, smoothed by water and time. In the distance, one formation looked like a replica of Edvard Munch's "The Scream."

Driving some more, we passed trees downed by wind and storms, their petrified roots punching angrily at the air. We stopped near an old homestead where we spotted a corral and an altar alongside an abandoned log cabin. On the other side of the cabin, a rickety wooden tripod leaned precariously over a stone firepit. In my mind, I saw women from an earlier time, dodging wafts of smoke as they cooked and swapped stories over an open fire.

A bit farther up the road, a woman practiced a yoga routine in an open expanse, stopping occasionally to take photos of the scenery from a camera perched on a nearby tripod. Her poses looked intricate, like Standing-Hand-to-Big-Toe and Nataranjasana (Dancer's Pose). She was agile and beautiful, and we tried not to make it obvious that we were watching.

Back in Santa Fe, we met up with Tim Lee, the best man from our wedding forty-three years earlier. He lived there part time back then. We invited him for a simple, affordable glass of wine in my own private Santa Fe sitting room. Instead, he suggested he treat us to dinner at the Luminaria Restaurant at Loretto.

Later that week, Tim drove us to Taos so that Rice could enjoy the view and not have to watch the road. I'm happy to report, Taos did *not* smell like urine. We enjoyed browsing for local art, and I picked up some turquoise quartz bookends to remember our trip. After lunch at the Orlando, we stopped by the lovely San Jose de Gracia Catholic Church in Las Trampas, where Tim snapped our picture.

Before we left Santa Fe, we visited Tim's lovely home on a ridge about a mile up from the Plaza. We drank extremely good wine and enjoyed his collection of pottery and art, including some handcrafted miniature Southwestern horses. The view from his place at twilight was amazing.

Back in Georgia, a recurring question lingered so I asked Rice what he thought.

"Is it odd I want to revisit all these people who touched our lives along the way?"

He smiled. "I think it's a pretty natural thing to want to do at this stage in our lives."

I suppose. Then again, meeting up with old friends like Tim often raises the question: Would we strike up a similar friendship if we met today?

Twenty years ago, it would have bothered me to say, "Possibly not." Today, I'm less idealistic. So much of how we meet the folks who touch our lives is circumstantial. It's based on where we are on our individual journeys. Once upon a time, Tim and Rice were college grad assistants and roommates, two debaters who lived in squalid housing and often dined on rice and cream-of-something soup. I inherited Tim as part of the package when I started to see Rice, and I'm glad I did.

As I write this, Tim is a single but newly engaged; Rice and I have been married all our lives. Tim still works as a prominent Houston attorney, his specialty, civil appellate law. Rice and I have retired; our work these days (his, at least) mostly involves doting on our grandchildren. Chances are, if we hadn't known Tim from years ago, our paths would never cross now.

But that's not the point.

The point is, we *did* connect back in the day. That bond enriched us. And somewhere inside, it's still part of who we are today.

Revisiting memories made and lessons learned thus far:

- Favorite wrong turn: Learning the GPS on the iPhone has a walk mode. Who knew??

- Travel tip gleaned: As much as you can, make time to stop and explore a quaint stretch of highway or visit a small town full of eclectic art and people who move at a slower pace.

- Insight into marriage . . . and life: Friendships ebb and flow through the years. What's awesome is reaching an age when we stop comparing our lots and just focus on how our bonds touched our lives along the way.

Chapter 22: Winding Our Way Through the Constitution State

2022: Connecticut

In July 2022, Rice suggested we visit Connecticut. It would be our forty-sixth state. And our forty-third anniversary.

"Yes!" I pumped a fist into the air. "Finally, I'll get to taste Leona's secret sauce!"

He groaned, perhaps at my corny reference to the movie *Mystic Pizza*. But more likely he recalled our plans to visit Mystic years earlier, on the tail end of our trip to see Daniel and Lauren when they lived in Providence.

A friend from work had recommended we drive a bit down the coast into Connecticut to a town called Mystic. "The pizza there is to die for," she said.

"Are you serious?" I'd always loved the Julia Roberts coming-of-age movie about three teenaged girls who slung pizza and learned about life during the summer after their high school graduation. But could its pizza really be all that good?

"It's definitely worth the drive," my friend promised.

We never made it to Mystic during that trip, our only visit to Daniel and Lauren's place before they left Rhode Island.

But back to Connecticut. I'd been lusting to sample Leona's secret sauce in Mystic for six years now. A trip to the Constitution State, to one of the thirteen original colonies, would also allow us to check one more off the list of our Fifty-State Project.

We landed in Hartford, famished and irritated that our rental car didn't contain a print map of the state. (It's the little things, you know?) Not sure what restaurants we might (or might not) find near our hotel, we opted for lunch at a little Guatemalan place we spotted enroute. After lunch, which was good, we drove to the Homewood Suites on the outskirts of Manchester, the *correct* hotel this time. Of course, we still hit a snag. Our room wasn't ready.

Instead of just waiting around for our room, we drove around Hartford to get a peek at the capitol and check out the Mark Twain House. Again, walk-up tickets had been replaced by reservation-only slots, a post-pandemic practice we kept forgetting about. In other words, we didn't get inside. But we did get to leer up at the massive Lego statue of Twain in the lobby. We also enjoyed walking the grounds, with islands of lilies in bloom beneath massive trees that provided shade from the hot summer sun.

When we finally checked into our hotel, I was a bit disappointed. The place had a Manchester address, and it overlooked a failing mall. Our room itself didn't exactly ooze with New England charm. It was clean and spacious, though. While we unpacked, Rice ignored any pissiness I might have let slip through and suggested we drive away from our hotel area and into downtown Manchester for dinner. Good call on his part.

Manchester's small-town eclectic vibe lifted my spirits. A cocktail at the Urban Lodge didn't hurt, I'm sure. Then back outside, I spotted a lofty angel, painted on brick, looking up toward the heavens, her eyes filled with hope. She was surrounded by pink and white roses and splatters of turquoise and black paint. Beside her, towering words told us where we were: *Silk City – Downtown Manchester.*

Ah. I'd found a mural, painted on a rustic old building. Rice stood by patiently as I stopped to photograph it. Meanwhile, a woman walked up behind us.

"Would you like to take an off-hours tour of Workspace?" she asked. "It's right around the corner. We're currently featuring works by artists fighting addiction."

"Sure," Rice and I agreed in unison.

The gallery consisted of individual work nooks, a commons area, and hundreds of annotated works. They lined the walls like a patchwork quilt.

We perused the art while the woman left us to tend to other business. One particularly haunting oil depicted the face of a man. Messy and matted dark hair framed his face, and his eyes shone with fear tinged with hope. The emotion behind the face in the painting moved me. Its title? *Self Portrait.*

When we finished touring the Workspace, we thanked the woman for the unique experience and headed to Crazy Taco for dinner. We sat near a dad having dinner with his nine-year-old son old. Based on their discussion, which we overheard, we gleaned they, too, were on a mission to visit all fifty states.

"We're on state forty-six ourselves," Rice told them.

"We hope to cover eighteen states this summer," the dad said.

My eyes widened. "That's wild."

For a moment, I wondered, what was their hurry? It wasn't my business, and I didn't ask. Dad might be divorced and trying to fit in father-son travels whenever he could. Or worse, he might be sick and trying to make the most of the time he had left. Or maybe they just loved to travel and finally had the time.

Whatever the case, I wished them safe travels. I squeezed Rice's hand on the way back to our car, feeling just a bit guilty I'd been so ugly about our own travels a few hours earlier.

· ♥ ·

Rice wanted to drive to New Haven and check out Yale while we were here.

"Our second Ivy," he said, reminding me that our first had been Brown.

We drove around town, gawking at old gabled houses on tree-lined residential streets. On the main drag, gorgeous old churches and classroom buildings predominated. We passed a brick storefront displaying its Lululemon goods. Nearby, a street vendor hawked Jack's All Beef Hot Dogs.

Before moving on, we drove through an antiquated graveyard, its gray and white stones erect behind black iron fence rails. Some of the markers had aged beyond legibility, but I made out one for a Revolutionary War captain who died in May 1784. So much history laid out before us at every turn.

We took a longer route on our drive from New Haven to Mystic, my love of small towns demanding a short detour to explore Guilford. Immediately, I felt like we'd found Stars Hollow, the quaint TV town *The Gilmore Girls* called home in the early 2000s. Purple hydrangeas popped in front of a yellow storefront at the local apothecary. A brick paved alleyway led us to cafes and shops, as well as a rustic old diner. It sold fresh flowers, baked goods, and deli items for picnics on the town green.

Oh, and just in case anyone's wondering . . .

We *did* finally make it to Mystic, a town that delighted me even more than I expected. Picture a seaport New England village with charming shops, maritime décor, and a real-life drawbridge. And a place called Mystic Pizza, where we sat in a booth beneath pictures with scenes from the movie.

After taking a bite of our pie, I immediately thought of the movie, the part where "The Fireside Gourmet" unexpectedly visits the restaurant. He takes a bite or two, and with no sign of expression on his face, jots some notes in his notebook before paying and leaving. A few days later, when the Fireside Gourmet's latest show airs, he gives the restaurant his highest rating and calls the pizza "superb."

I tend to agree. The pizza was damned good.

As our Connecticut trip started to wind down, I turned to Pinterest (again!) to help plan an itinerary. I read about a loop that was home to some waterfalls and wineries.

"Sounds good," Rice said, following the instructions on our GPS, which took us to a patch of forest along a creek with a tiny waterfall. Had we arrived at Buttermilk Falls? Or were we at some obscure place in the woods? Only one other hiker and his dog trudged the sloping rocks that framed the water. What the heck? Wherever we were, it was beautiful, and we enjoyed it.

Our GPS did us proud again, taking us to a winery. I think it was Hopkins Vineyards, but I forgot to take a picture of the sign on our way in.

We shared small talk with a couple who had brought their small baby out for a day trip.

"I hear the traffic is pretty tough in Atlanta," the husband mused.

"It's definitely faster," I said.

The wife tucked a pacifier into their baby's mouth as he lounged in the nearby stroller. Then she looked me straight in the eye. "Atlanta's traffic may move faster," she said, "but don't be fooled. Connecticut has its own strain of crazy drivers."

After leaving the winery, we drove to Kent Falls State Park, where I did remember to take pictures. Videos, actually. I posted a sweet little section of trickling water on Facebook before we found a more robust section of falls. Before I could update my post, a Facebook buddy familiar with where we were made a comment: "Seems like those falls have fizzled some through the years."

Oof. I posted an updated picture, showing a more robust section of the falls.

But speaking of fizzle . . . That's exactly what happened to our Internet connection when we left the falls. Why mention this? Because no Internet meant no GPS. And our rental car had no paper map, as I've mentioned. On top of all that, Rice's excellent sense of direction had taken a sabbatical. After several false starts and some backtracking, Rice finally got us on track on the Interstate back to the hotel.

Tired and crabby, I groused, "I'm kind of over traveling. I just want to go home.

I sensed Rice felt cranky, too, mostly because he was so quiet. We rode without talking for some time.

"Whoa!" he exclaimed suddenly, breaking the silence "There's something you don't see every day."

"What?"

Rice pointed to the other side of the Interstate where, sure enough, an odd scene was unfolding.

"What in the world?" I squinted to see better. "Is that what I think it is?"

"If you're seeing a car driving on the shoulder, yes."

"But it's going the wrong way," I pointed out.

"Actually," Rice corrected me, "its nose is headed in the right direction. But it's driving in reverse."

"And incredibly fast."

Wow. Eventually, the scene was but a memory in our rearview mirror.

"The lady at the winery was right," I said after a beat. "Connecticut definitely does have its own strain of crazy drivers."

Seeing that crazy Connecticut driver in action got our adrenaline pumping enough to wake us up for another experience. Good thing, too, as it was the date of our actual anniversary.

We opted to visit West Hartford, a lively entertainment district, and we chose to eat dinner at an upscale place with outdoor seating.

As we enjoyed an appetizer and a drink, a younger couple across from us caught our attention. They had finished their meal, and she made a bit of a show about pulling out her credit card when the check arrived. Then, as they waited to get her card back, she got up and walked around the table and sat on his lap, face to face, straddle-style.

Keep in mind, they couldn't have been more than four or five feet away from us.

"Whoa," I said. "Looks like somebody's getting lucky tonight!"

Rice shot me a look that said, *Oh, my God. Did you just say that out loud?*

I did. Not that I'm proud of myself. It's just, sometimes I have no filter. Things come spouting from my mouth before I fully think about them. I sometimes remind Rice that perhaps he'll choose more wisely the next time around.

"If I die," I've told him more than once, "I suspect you'll re-marry and choose a flat-chested, long-legged brunette who has a bit more class than your first wife."

And he's responded the same way every time, "Jan, I'd be bored to death."

As we approached the car after dinner, Rice said, "I think that was the best meal I've had since we've been here."

"It was very good," I agreed. (And, no, I don't recall what we had as I write this.)

But then I thought back to *Mystic Pizza,* which also served an incredibly good meal, one that I actually remembered. Yet it wasn't the food I was thinking about. It was a line from the movie, the one where JoJo muses: "What the hell *do* you think Leona really puts in that pizza?"

Sometimes, when I think about long-term relationships like my marriage, I paraphrase that question to ponder: What the hell really *is* behind it all?

I don't profess to know the answer. But I do know this: I always follow the question with a knock on wood . . . and a silent teensy weensy hex on flat-chested, long-legged brunette women who might cross Rice's path after I'm gone.

It's not that I don't wish the Riceman a second chance at some happiness. I do.

But part of me wouldn't mind if his prediction proved to be true: without me around, he'd be pretty damned bored.

· ♥ ·

Revisiting memories made and lessons learned thus far:

- Favorite wrong turn: Taking so long to get to Mystic, which was well worth the wait.

- Travel tip gleaned: When a local tells you to watch for their state's own strain of crazies out on the road, believe them. You never know what you might encounter.

- Insight into marriage . . .and life: Tell your spouse life wouldn't be the same without them. (If you think it would be even better, don't mention that part.)

Chapter 23: Exploring the Flickertail, Mount Rushmore & Bonanza States

2023: The Dakotas ~ Montana

As Rice and I neared the end of our Fifty-State Project, we made plans to see the Dakotas and Montana—destinations forty-seven, forty-eight, and forty-nine. Prices to fly and also rent a car gave me heart palpitations. Granted, I didn't fully consider all the costs of taking a 4,200-mile trip in a ten-year-old Passat. Still, I sold the idea to Rice like this: "We've always enjoyed our road trips together. Plus, if we drive, we can visit long-time friends on each leg of the journey."

Another concern niggled at the back of my mind. It may sound silly, but . . . I fretted some about making a trip through beef country because, well, it was beef country. Six months earlier, Rice had adopted a vegan diet, cutting out all meat and fish, plus foods made with eggs, milk, and cheese. In my mind, this was vegetarianism on steroids. In his mind, "It's just plant-based eating, and it's easy. If a food comes from something that has lips, I don't eat it."

Okay. But we were heading into *beef* country. Rice had always *loved* beef, but now he was following this plant-based food plan more by choice (in my mind) than necessity (in his mind). His original cardiologist had put him on a Mediterranean diet, but his new cardiologist said, "Not good enough. A vegan plan would be better."

God love my husband; he heard an order in what I would consider a suggestion.

I am not anti-veganism, but I suggested he compromise on this trip. You know, maybe enjoy a bite of meat here or there. But Rice would have none of that. He'd lost tons of weight on his new regimen. He liked his new lifestyle. Why was I making such a big deal of it?

I might have been able to let it go, if not for this: HE CHEATED.

No, he didn't let meat or cheese touch his lips. Still, he was only quasi-vegan. What else would you call it when he made this one major exception to the rules? HE ATE DONUTS.

Do you know what most donuts contain? Eggs and milk. I may be no Einstein, but I'm pretty sure eggs and milk come from creatures that have lips.

Even today, I marvel at how my quasi-vegan could take a 4,200-mile road trip through *beef* country, pass up deep-fried beef cubes and elk and big fat medium-rare steaks, but insist on seeking out donuts. Donuts, for pity's sake. Through all three states, he sniffed out every bakery, strip mall, and diner in search of donuts.

Was I bitter? Hells, yes, I was. Especially when he continued to lose weight.

· ♥ ·

The first leg of our trek took us to Evansville, Indiana. Immediately on entering town, a gaggle of glee-filled youths in wheelchairs raced toward us on the other side of the road. Smiles streaked their faces, and their hair and jackets billowed free in the breeze.

"Am I seeing things?" I murmured to Rice.

Turns out I wasn't. Our hotel sat around the corner from the Neurodevelopmental Center of Southwestern Indiana, serving youth with autism, intellectual or other mental health issues, and developmental disabilities. I loved seeing these young folks living life with such zest.

Evansville delighted us with its walkable downtown, a bar that served perfect Manhattans and lavender-lemon martinis, and a nearby diner in a little brick walk-up that dished up Southeastern Asian food with plenty of vegan options. I'd heard very little about the town before our visit, but I became a fast fan.

Before leaving the next day, we drove to Boss Field (where parts of the Tom Hanks version of *A League of Their Own* was filmed). We didn't make it onto the field. Unfortunately, the gate was locked. But we *did* manage to make a stop at the Donut Bank. Yes, indeed. The search for the perfect donut began that very first morning.

From Evanston, we drove to Pewaukee, Wisconsin, to spend a delightful evening with my former college roommate and maid of honor, Lyn Owziak. I could tell you we had a blast with Lyn and her husband, Doug—we did—and that it felt like very little time had passed—so true. For the sake of moving on with our travel stories, let's just say: What happened in Pewaukee will stay in Pewaukee.

From Pewaukee, we headed toward Madison. You might remember that, in late 1979, I got a wild hair that Rice and I should relocate from Boulder to Madison, sight unseen? That impetuous move never happened, but I still wanted to see the town.

Turns out we saw less of it than we thought we would.

On the outskirts of Madison, I asked Rice, "Do you hear that?"

"Do I hear what?"

"A knocking sound coming from underneath the Passat on my side."

He listened for a moment. "I don't think so."

The noise persisted.

"Well . . . maybe?" Rice admitted.

For a bit, we bounced back and forth between choosing to ignore the noise and convincing each other that it was nothing.

Finally, just to be safe, we pulled into the Zimbrick Volkswagen Dealership that happened to be ahead on our left.

If you're thinking nothing beats starting a looooong road trip with car issues, you're right. No worries, though. Ninety minutes and $200 later, we left the dealership with a patched drive shaft cover *and* enough time to check out Madison's lakes—Wingra, Mendota, and Monona. Oh, we also stopped at the Greenbush Bakery, where we sampled the biggest apples fritters ever. (I think fritters might be donuts' cousins, but who knows?)

Driving the bypass around St. Paul, Minnesota, took two hours. Ugh! When we arrived in Fargo, North Dakota, it was bigger than I'd expected. And very charming. We hiked around town, looking for murals along Art Alley, until we learned that Art Alley was not in Fargo but rather in Bismarck. Sigh. While still in Fargo, we came across a gigantic mural of Bob Dylan. Go figure. Dylan's a Minnesota boy, but we still photographed the incredible mural of him before hitting the road again.

From Fargo we drove to Bismarck, and we *did* find Art Alley there. Many of its murals paid tribute to a time when bison roamed the plains, and Native Americans ruled the land. The commissioned murals brightened the alley *and* told a history that shouldn't be forgotten. Native Americans lived here first, and the white folks stole their land and treated them in abysmal ways.

Our next stop was Dickinson, where gray clouds threatened a major storm as we approached. An electrical outage left our hotel—and half the town—without power and sent us all to Phat Fish Brewing for dinner. We ordered a new-to-us Detroit-style pizza with the largest crust I've ever seen, let alone eaten. (And remember, I'm from Michigan.)

After dinner, the storm had cleared, and we drove around Dickinson's flat roads that crisscrossed in neat little grids. We opted to stay in Dickinson over Medora, thinking the latter looked a bit kvetchy. In hindsight, Medora was cute and walkable, with pickleball courts for adults and a playground replicating the town in miniature for kids.

I've heard North Dakotans grow tired of hearing their state is the last of the contiguous U.S. that many folks visit. Not gonna lie. The Flickertail State didn't call to me either, at least not the way that other states have. Yet the next day, as we drove a loop of Teddy Roosevelt National Park, I had a revelation. Even though I think it's wrong to have favorites, except for husbands, North Dakota was pushing its way to the top of a list I had no desire to make.

Barely a half-hour into the park, the drastic change in terrain struck me. Colorful rocks and scenic views stretched out all around us. Along the roadway, massive, majestic bison stopped traffic, scowling and snorting and shaking off flies as they crossed the roads whenever they chose to do so. Experiencing nature this way made me feel small, but in the loveliest of ways. There's an indescribable solace to being just a speck of dust in the wind. Somehow, I understood how Roosevelt found peace in this place, even after losing his wife during childbirth the same day his mother died from typhoid.

· ♥ ·

Rice and I almost didn't visit the Bonanza State on this trip. We knew we wouldn't have time to see the western half of Montana, with its beautiful mountain ranges we'd heard so much about. Still, we decided to see what we could, focusing on the eastern half of the state with its prairie terrain and badlands.

So, what did we think of Billings? We liked it. During our travels throughout the states, we've enjoyed seeking out public arts projects, like murals or painted sculptures of things that represent the area. For instance, we looked for painted bears in New Bern, North Carolina, and sought out multi-colored giant hands in Berea, Kentucky. In Montana, at least in Billings, the sculptures were longhorn steer. I should also give a tip of the hat to the awesome vegan-friendly restaurant (Walker's) we discovered near our hotel. Who woulda thunk it?

In addition to Billings, we visited Little Bighorn near Crow Agency while still in Montana. Sometimes the earth speaks to me in ways the history books never did. This was one of those times. Looking out over the vast open plains, at the ridges and ravines and the stark white markers that honor the dead, stirred something inside me.

Fewer than three hundred lives were lost during the Battle of Little Bighorn, once known as Custer's Last Stand. Two hundred fifty-nine of Custer's men and an estimated thirty-one from the Cheyenne and Lakota tribes died.

The Native Americans fought to retaliate for how the white man continued to welch on land promises, kill off the bison, and desecrate their world. I get that. Yet I can't help but mourn for both sides. Custer wasn't the only member of his family to die during the battle. I believe two brothers, a brother-in-law, and a nephew were also slain.

Getting ready to leave, I was reminded that too many parents, widows and widowers, and children get left behind at war time.

Taking one last look at the vast expanse all around me, I couldn't help but notice that nothing is quite so blue as a Montana sky.

Those are some of the thoughts that crossed my mind when I visited Little Bighorn.

· ♥ ·

Our last official leg of the trip began in Deadwood, South Dakota, where we stayed at the Bullock Hotel. To my disappointment, Sheriff Seth Bullock's ghost never showed himself. In fact, the only ghost we encountered belonged to Coca-Cola, which was completely scarce in favor of Pepsi.

Deadwood's entire downtown is an historic site, once home to such folks as Wyatt Earp and Al Swearengen, a saloon owner and pimp who controlled the town's opium trade. It provided a lot of fun, like reenactments of gun fights outside the saloons. Truth be told, it was even more kvetchy than we feared Madera might be.

We visited Mt. Rushmore, which was physically impressive, but after seeing it, that was it. The Crazy Horse Monument and Museum, on the other hand, showcased beautiful art and education displays throughout the museum. I learned that the Iroquois were a matriarchal society, where women headed lodges and appointed the Chiefs. (But if you guessed that the Chiefs were still men, you'd be right.) Sadly, the Crazy Horse statue itself remains unfinished, over seventy years after carving first began. No estimated date for completion has been set.

In South Dakota's Black Hills, we followed the breathtaking Needles Highway. Its massive granite needles lined the roads and lead to the pristine Sylvan Lake. Along the way, we took a detour for some tastings at Prairie Berry Winery, home of the infamous Red Ass Rhubarb wine. I tried a lavender cider—so good!—and then after our flights, we moved on for a tasting at the brewery next door.

Once back in Deadwood, we visited the Mount Moriah Cemetery, where Wild Bill Hickock and Calamity Jane lay in rest. A tour bus stopped near us, and the guide pointed out where the cemetery's Jewish and Chinese sections were, along with a special area for children, and a potter's field where paupers and indigent people were buried. This segregation in burial grounds made me pause. I didn't exactly love what it said about our world.

Back near the Bullock Hotel, mule deer grazed in a forested area above the road. We watched for a bit as dusk set in. Then we retired to our room, to be well rested for the long ride ahead.

· ❤ ·

Revisiting memories made and lessons learned thus far:

- Favorite wrong turn: Discovering a "new" Midwest and Great Plains region where beef isn't necessarily what's always for dinner.

- Travel tip gleaned: If you travel with a donut aficionado and join the search for THE BEST of THE BEST in every town visited, don't expect the scale to like you once you return home.

- Insight into marriage . . .and life: Try not to fret about the things your partner is or isn't eating. And remember, mama donuts don't have lips.

Chapter 24: The Last Frontier – Ahhh!

2023: Alaska

Warmed by the July sunshine sparkling off the harbor water, Rice and I toasted each other on our stateroom balcony. Our ship, Cunard's Queen Elizabeth II, was leaving Vancouver, Canada for Alaska. For better or worse, we chose to visit this final destination of our Fifty-State Project by way of a ten-day cruise.

Remember what happened during our three-generation family cruise to the Virgin Islands in 2016? Well, despite that calamity, we stepped out of our comfort zone here, electing to try another cruise. What can I say? On the tail of our 4,200-mile road trip through Montana and the Dakotas, we were ready to let someone else take the helm. Not to mention, the Cunard's state room sure beat the interior of a Passat.

We opted to travel with two other couples, which is unusual for us. My cousin Beth and her husband Sam, whom we visited previously in Idaho, invited us to join them. They also invited my cousin Gary and his wife Natalie. I'd never met Natalie. Shoot, I barely remembered Gary, having last seen him when I was around five years old.

Let me explain. I was born Janet Putnam and lost my dad to an accident when I was seventeen months old. My mom remarried shortly afterward, and I got folded into Harold Heidrich's family, with two older stepsisters and, eventually, two younger half-sisters. I loved visiting my Grandma Putt (as everyone called her) when I was little. But she died when I was in the fifth or sixth grade, and more and more, I lost touch with that side of my family.

"I'm a little nervous about this trip," I told Rice a few days before our departure.

"Don't be," he said. "Even if you don't mesh with family, we'll still have Alaska."

How right he was. Alaska more than delivered, starting with great weather—a week of high temperatures in the sixties and only one afternoon spittle of rain.

We sailed into Sitka first, where snowcapped mountains towered behind the historic downtown, all of it framed against ocean water that shone like crystal. We enjoyed the town's rich Russian heritage, evident in the architecture all around us, but especially during our stop into St. Michael's Cathedral. Other Sitka excitement included a visit to Old Harbor Books (for me, of course). And then "someone" among us couldn't resist the sign to try Ernie's Old Time Saloon special, a Duck Fart (equal parts Kahlua, Bailey's, and Crown Royal).

Next came Skagway, ruggedly beautiful but rife with a few wrong turns of our own making. We'd long been told to take the train to White Pass Summit for the most breathtaking views of a lifetime. When we checked an online booking site, it showed the train to be sold out. Disappointed, we opted to take the bus instead. Later, we learned from Natalie that train seats were available through the cruise line.

As our bus tickets were nonrefundable, I told the others to snag up some train seats without us and enjoy. They did, which made me a bit envious but also assured me that we could travel just fine with these folks. We could do our own thing much of the time, then meet up for pre-dinner cocktails and compare potential adventures for that evening and the following day.

Skagway's bus trip wasn't a total bust. We captured plenty of photos of breathless vistas during frequent stops. On the downside, the tour took up much of the day, leading us to miss out on trying the famous and ginormous Klondike Doughboys. These plate-sized pieces of fry bread are served up with crispy edges and puffy innards, completely doused in cinnamon sugar for days. I'm guessing they taste as good as they smell, but we'll never know.

After a large breakfast, we passed on a doughboy that morning, and the shop had closed by the time the bus rolled back into town. I thought Rice would be crushed, but he just shrugged. (And he calls me the unpredictable one?)

In Juneau, we walked around downtown for a bit, then found a quaint outside cafe area. Rice had a vegetarian wrap from the Alaskan Crepe Escape, and I enjoyed blackened rockfish tacos from Deckhand Dave's. (Double thumbs up for both.)

After lunch, we hopped on the Goldbelt Mount Roberts Tramway. At $50 a pop, I had hoped the ride would be scenic and comfortable. Wrong. Tramway staff packed us into a car as if we were sardines, and another set of staff hustled us off at the top for a touristy stop of shopping, snacks, and beer. I was already feeling a bit testy when Rice asked if I'd like to hike up the trail to the site of Father Brown's Cross.

"How far up is it?" I narrowed my eyes at him.

Affable as always, he shrugged. Then he added, "What'd'ya say?"

What I say now is, "Holy shit, we did it!" (If I recall the actual day of the hike, I might have whined, "I want a divorce," right before we reached the fifteen-foot cross near the summit.)

Truth is, I've grown accustomed to the ebb and flow in our approach to adventure. We've each learned when to push a little bit more. And when to back down.

Father Brown's Cross was a worthy push on his part. I'm still not sure the trek was only a "one-mile loop," as I've seen it described in my post-trip Google searches. It took for-freaking-ever, but it led to a place that bald eagles call home. Massive totem poles hugged the path's edge, along with tribal etchings on the ancient trees. From the site of Father Brown's Cross, we could see downtown Juneau with all the cruise ships moored around it, surrounded by gorgeous mountain peaks and clear blue skies.

I'm grateful we took that hellish hike up the mountainside, rife with its mighty steep switchbacks that almost ended our marriage. I'm even more thankful the trek down the mountain was less strenuous. I slept like a baby that night, tucked in a comfy king-sized bed next to Rice, rocking back and forth on the ocean as we sailed toward Glacier Bay National Park.

The next day, we watched a pilot boat pull up beside our ship so a marine pilot could use a rope ladder to climb aboard. That's how I learned that expert marine pilots board large cruise ships to safely guide passage around straits and icebergs in places like Alaska. They navigate by memory—something I thankfully didn't realize during our cruise as I'm sure it would have made me nervous.

I found it magical, cruising by mountains of snow and ice floes past Hubbard Glacier and into Glacier Bay National Park. True, folks who'd visited in the past lamented how much the glaciers have shrunk. And while I like to think I might have seen a whale in the distance, I'm not sure I did. (Rice, of course, is quite positive he saw one.)

A couple more ports awaited us after our passage through the glaciers. To say the towns started to look alike would be unfair because they all have their own unique charm. The landscape of Icy Strait Point, for instance, is lined with trees dripping with what looks like Spanish moss, and its beaches are lined with sand.

In Ketchikan, walking the Creek Street boardwalk took us past galleries, boutiques, and gift shops. The town still celebrates what was once its famous red-light district. The sign for "Dolly's House – Where Both Men and Salmon Came Upstream to Spawn" is just one example. I enjoyed learning about the town's history—and a bit about the salmon industry. But to me, its crowning glory was the creek itself, which churned underneath the stilted boardwalk, winding along a path rich with nature and culture, history and art.

I'd be remiss if I didn't include a little something about the Queen Elizabeth II herself. For starters, I fell in love with, and still miss, her two-floor library, with its winding staircase and beautiful stained glass stretched atop dark, rich wooden shelves. I'm sure it goes without saying, but I loved its books and newspapers and little nooks for sneaking in quiet time for oneself.

It's hard to choose which way I preferred to start each morning: hot coffee and pastries delivered to our stateroom and enjoyed on the balcony overlooking the water. Or going to breakfast in the dining room for the best Eggs Benedict I've ever tasted. Many of the folks cruising the QE came from Britain, so meeting them over breakfast was a delight.

On sea days, we came to enjoy some of the ship's daily activities, like high tea mid-afternoon, followed by trivia at four. Those Brits that delighted us at breakfast often kicked our booties at trivia, beating us out with pop culture questions pertaining to British TV shows.

One of the things that surprised me most is how much I enjoyed the ship's two formal dinner nights. I'm not big on pomp and ceremony, but something about dressing for dinner—maybe seeing the Riceman in a tux?—warmed my heart.

I enjoyed all of our dinners, even our first one, when I managed to spill a glass of red wine down the front of Rice's shirt and jacket. It was a full glass too. I'm not quite sure how it happened, but Rice was a good sport, and my faux pas sure broke the ice with my long-lost family.

Speaking of family (on the Putnam side, that is), I've mentioned before that Beth's never met a stranger. Almost immediately, I also felt a comfortable connection with Gary. His dad and my dad were brothers. Being five years my senior, he remembered things that I didn't.

For starters, he told me, "Your dad and Beth's dad"—the youngest two brothers of the Putnam clan—"used to toss me around when I was little just like a football."

I smiled as I envisioned that picture of the family I never really knew.

"Another story," Gary continued. "Your dad was not a big guy. But he was strong. And Beth's dad [Uncle Keith] had a mouth on him." Gary's eyes twinkled, and so did Beth's. "Sometimes Keith would be out at the bars, talk trash to someone, and then get the snot beat out of him." Gary paused. "But the next night, Keith would take your dad back to the bar to even the score."

Oh . . . I was a little mortified to hear that, but also a bit tickled.

What can I say? Isn't the point of sharing our stories to create emotional connections, the kind that move us toward real understanding? Not just of others, but of ourselves as well.

On the last night of our cruise, I snuggled up to Rice.

"Can you believe we've completed our Fifty-State Project?" I whispered.

He laughed softly. "Despite some wrong turns along the way."

From Curley's Motel in Paradise to a stateroom on the Queen Elizabeth II . . . what a journey we've shared. Somehow, I think those wrong turns got us precisely to where we're supposed to be.

• ♥ •

Revisiting memories made and lessons learned thus far:

- Favorite wrong turn: Cruising again, despite our 2016 debacle. This time was so much better.

- Travel tip gleaned: If you've dressed extra fancy for dinner, opt for white wine, not red.

- Insight into marriage . . . and life: Sometimes wrong turns get you precisely to where you're supposed to be.

Afterword

F rom Rice

"YOU don't know about me without you have read a book by the name of The Adventures of Tom Sawyer; but that ain't no matter. That book was made by Mr. Mark Twain, and he told the truth, mainly. There was things which he stretched, but mainly he told the truth." The Adventures of Huckleberry Finn ~ Samuel Clemens

I grew up in Central Illinois farm country. My parents were very young (twenty-one and seventeen) when I was born. My dad supported our family by working a factory job. My mother was a homemaker, never learning to drive. Money was tight and we never took vacations. Vacation pay went to cover bills or purchase a needed item. Until my wedding, the only time my family had been out of Central Illinois was to visit family in Milwaukee. The six-hour drive to Saginaw, Michigan, for our wedding took them two days.

So how did I learn to love travel?

It started with my love of geography and history. I would read books checked out from our local Carnegie Library. I'd read about ancient and faraway places and dream of not just visiting but actually living in some of them. I wanted to see the world.

Many folks would have joined the military after high school to see the world. I graduated during the middle of the Vietnam War so a stint in the military didn't appeal to me.

Instead, I accepted a scholarship to Illinois State University to participate in intercollegiate debate. Representing my school gave me the chance to travel the country to places I wouldn't have been able to do on my own: California, New York, Washington D.C.

From Illinois State, I went on to graduate school at Central Michigan University, where I fell in love with the department undergraduate secretary. In my eyes, she had traveled widely: Montreal, Hawaii, and France. She was so urbane.

Flash forward to forty-five plus years of marriage to that one-time undergrad secretary: Jan has tolerated my travel follies and allowed my love for travel to grow and mature. Somewhere along the journey, our roles reversed. I became the experienced world wanderer and she, the more hesitant homebody.

Somehow, we've made it work. As Jan indicated, I traveled alone many a time but never enjoyed it as much as just doing a road trip with her. Sharing a new dining experience...viewing vistas I had only dreamed about...standing in a place that I could only imagine from my boyhood reading...all these things are sweeter traveling with the love of my life.

I constantly look for opportunities for us to pack our bags and hit the road. I hope that you, dear reader, do too.

"Sometimes the light's all shinin' on me;
Other times I can barely see;
Lately it occurs to me
What a long, strange trip it's been."
~ Grateful Dead

From Jan

Do I look forward to travel the way that Rice does? Oh, hellz, no! Often, when he proposes a trip, I want to say to him, "Can't we just stay home already? Puh-leez!"

Yet throughout our marriage, our travels—whether to half a world away or barely beyond our back door—have enriched our lives, individually and as a couple. Travel has played an integral part in our journey. It's reminded us to value life over possessions. It's shaped our values, views, and even how we look at our marriage and family.

The amazing thing to me is that we survived the journey together *despite* our differences. Forty-five plus years in, we've visited all fifty states, and we're still doing life—and travel—together. (Knock on wood!) Our destinations and lodging preferences have changed through the years, depending on shifts in income, our kids' ages, and where we are on our separate career and retirement paths.

If I'm honest, what I often enjoy most about travel is looking back on it after it's over! So many memories. And the stories! Are they all special enough that I think the whole world will be dying to read them? Not at all. But here's the thing: they're special to us.

So, while I hope this book entertains you, my bigger wish is that you'll let our stories serve as a bridge to sharing your own . . . with family, friends, and loved ones. If you don't share them, who will?

Remember, dear reader, stories matter. They're important to share, and there's no right or wrong way to do it.

Yet come to think of it, even if there is, you can only make one wrong turn at a time.

· ♥ ·

More from Jan

Thank you for reading *One Wrong Turn at a Time*. I hope you enjoyed it. If you did, I'd love for you to leave an online review on the platform(s) of your choice.

For another story about a woman on a journey, I invite you to enjoy:

SECRETS OF THE BLUE MOON by Jan Heidrich-Rice
. . . a lost love, a small-town mystery, and a ghost story.

Meet Marnie Putnam, a woman at a crossroads. Her marriage is dying, but a job in the quaint Georgia town of Lake Gardner may just bring her back to life . . . or death.

Recording the haunted history of this charming town reveals two shocking truths:

- Ghosts are real
- The blue moon holds deadly secrets

Will Marnie choose to return to the safety of her crumbling marriage . . . or risk death by using a new-found skill to unravel the town's mystery?

Secrets of the Blue Moon can be ordered from your book retailer of choice.

• ♥ •

Secrets of the Blue Moon is Book No. 1 in the Lake Gardner mystery series. It's been described as book club fiction that celebrates family, friendship, and small-town Southern living. (Psst, you'll also find a mystery, a pinch of romance, and a delicious dose of supernatural suspense in each book.)

Visit Jan's website to order books or learn more about her and her work:

www.janheidrichrice.com

Sign up for updates, occasional giveaways, and other surprises at:

www.janheidrichrice.com/contact

Acknowledgements

T his section is hard to write if only because I know I'll forget to include someone.

For starters, I'd like to thank my original critique group, the Thursday Night Slashers. It's been years since we met weekly to "slash" up each other's writing, but you encouraged me first, and for that I'm forever grateful. Thank you, Carol Ansardi, Cynthia Houston, Kathy (KB) Kincer, and Karen Kirkpatrick. And P.S. to you, Judy Shubert, please know that your memory is indeed a blessing.

To my current critique partners, Kimberly Hays de Muga and Katherine Caldwell, I appreciate how you weed through the sludge I send you every week to help me find structure, story, and truth. You guide me to know which work I should hone but also which I should trash. You take no bullshit, but you do it with kindness. I appreciate you so, so much.

Thank you to my growing writing community, including members of the Atlanta Writers Club, my own OWT Pub Buds, and the Women Fiction Writers Association. Special thanks to Kathryn (Kathy) Dodson for holding my hand through writing, marketing, and all the things that demand attention when launching a second book. You're da bomb. My gratitude also goes out to Lainey Cameron, Charlotte Dune, and the "gang" for welcoming me into your ongoing weekly writer support group. Even in fallow times of writing, you're such a light.

My professional team deserves huge thanks, starting with Elizabeth Mackey, who designs the greatest covers ever. To Brian Klems, thank you for holding my feet to the fire to make my work stronger through story. You are a task master, and I thank you for that. To Lori Diederich, please accept my thanks for laying your eagle eyes on my final copy. Any errors that slipped through are on me, not you.

Part of me feels I also should thank 2020. It threw a monkey wrench into everyone's world, even that of publishing. It seems that during quarantine, a zillion folks wrote a novel, producing a glut of fiction for agents and editors to review. It got me thinking: "Does the world really need another novel?" I hope the answer is YES, YES, YES, but I have to admit, the change of speed and course in getting a novel published nudged me to finish this book, then barely in progress. It actually might be more important—to my family, if to nobody else.

Speaking of family . . . thank you, thank you to Daniel, Lauren, Quinn, Patrick, Britton, Charli, Alex, and Rice. Also, thank you, dear sisters, Lynne (and husband Kim), Susan, Tina, and Lisa (and husband Mitch). I have loved being on this journey of life with you all, and I hope being part of my journey, here in this book, will bring you more smiles than heartburn.

Finally, thank you, dear reader, for taking the time to read! I appreciate you tuning in to my stories, and I hope you'll consider ways to share yours as well. They matter. As do you.

Discussion Questions

1. How much did you know about this book before picking it up? What surprised you the most about the book?

2. Did any part of this book strike a particular emotion in you? Which part and what emotion did the book make you feel?

3. How did the author's story make you reflect on your own life and experiences?

4. Why do you think the author wanted to tell their story? What do you think is the main thing they wanted you to come away from reading the book with?

5. Did this book make you want to travel more? Why or why not?

6. If you could transport yourself to one moment or location in the book, where would it be?

7. If you had unlimited funds for a long weekend away to somewhere you've never been, where would you go? Who would you take with you? What would you do?

8. Did you highlight or bookmark any passages from the book? Did you have any favorite quotes? If so, share and discuss.

9. From your point of view, what were the central themes of the book? How well do you think the author did at exploring them?

About the Author

J an Heidrich-Rice writes creative nonfiction that reflects on family and the wonder and humor of everyday life. She also writes book club fiction laced with what-ifs. Sometimes haunting, often funny, her work is always spiked with hope and heart. She lives with her husband near Atlanta.

Jan enjoys hearing from readers and loves to visit book clubs, locally or via Zoom. Reach out to her to join you for a meeting...or just to stay in touch:

https://jan@janheidrichrice.com

www.ingramcontent.com/pod-product-compliance
Lightning Source LLC
Chambersburg PA
CBHW031308120626
46554CB00001BA/332